THE FUTURE OF WARFARE

Geopolitical Trends and the Future of Warfare

The Changing Global Environment and Its Implications for the U.S. Air Force

RAPHAEL S. COHEN, EUGENIU HAN, AND ASHLEY L. RHOADES

RAND PROJECT AIR FORCE

Prepared for the United States Air Force
Approved for public release; distribution unlimited

For more information on this publication, visit www.rand.org/t/RR2849z2

Library of Congress Cataloging-in-Publication Data is available for this publication.
ISBN: 978-1-9774-0296-7

Published by the RAND Corporation, Santa Monica, Calif.

Cover: derrrek/Getty Images
Spine: combo1982/Getty Images, matejmo/Getty Images, StudioM1/Getty Images

Preface

Where will the next war occur? Who will fight in it? Why will it occur? How will it be fought? Researchers with RAND Project AIR FORCE's Strategy and Doctrine Program attempted to answer these questions about the future of warfare—specifically, those conflicts that will drive a U.S. and U.S. Air Force response—by examining the key geopolitical, economic, environmental, geographic, legal, informational, and military trends that will shape the contours of conflict between now and 2030. This report on geopolitical trends and the future of warfare is one of a series that grew out of this effort. The other reports in the series are

- Raphael S. Cohen et al., *The Future of Warfare in 2030: Project Overview and Conclusions* (RR-2849/1-AF)
- Forrest E. Morgan and Raphael S. Cohen, *Military Trends and the Future of Warfare: The Changing Global Environment and Its Implications for the U.S. Air Force* (RR-2849/3-AF)
- Howard J. Shatz and Nathan Chandler, *Global Economic Trends and the Future of Warfare: The Changing Global Environment and Its Implications for the U.S. Air Force* (RR-2849/4-AF)
- Shira Efron, Kurt Klein, and Raphael S. Cohen, *Environment, Geography, and the Future of Warfare: The Changing Global Environment and Its Implications for the U.S. Air Force* (RR-2849/5-AF)
- Bryan Frederick and Nathan Chandler, *Restraint and the Future of Warfare: The Changing Global Environment and Its Implications for the U.S. Air Force* (RR-2849/6-AF).

This volume examines six geopolitical trends by asking four key questions for each trend. First, what does research say about how this variable shapes the conduct of warfare? Second, how has this variable historically shaped the conduct of warfare, especially in the post–Cold War era? Third, how might this variable be expected to change through 2030? And finally, but perhaps most importantly, how might this variable affect the future of warfare in this time frame, especially as it relates to the U.S. armed forces and the U.S. Air Force in particular? By answering these questions, it is hoped that this report will paint a picture of how geopolitics will shape conflict over the next decade and beyond.

This research was sponsored by the Director of Strategy, Concepts and Assessments, Deputy Chief of Staff for Strategic Plans and Requirements (AF/A5S). It is part of a larger study, entitled *The Future of Warfare*, that assists the Air Force in assessing trends in the future strategic environment for the next Air Force strategy. This report should be of value to the national security community and interested members of the general public, especially those with an interest in how global trends will affect the conduct of warfare. Comments are welcome and should be sent to the authors, Raphael S. Cohen, Eugeniu Han, and Ashley L. Rhoades. Research was completed in October 2018.

RAND Project AIR FORCE

RAND Project AIR FORCE (PAF), a division of the RAND Corporation, is the U.S. Air Force's federally funded research and development center for studies and analyses. PAF provides the Air Force with independent analyses of policy alternatives affecting the development, employment, combat readiness, and support of current and future air, space, and cyber forces. Research is conducted in four programs: Force Modernization and Employment; Manpower, Personnel, and Training; Resource Management; and Strategy and Doctrine. The research reported here was prepared under contract FA7014-16-D-1000.

Additional information about PAF is available on our website: www.rand.org/paf.

This report documents work originally shared with the U.S. Air Force on September 7, 2018. The draft report, issued in September 2018, was reviewed by formal peer reviewers and U.S. Air Force subject-matter experts.

Contents

Figures and Tables

Figures

Tables

Summary

Carl von Clausewitz famously argued that "war is the continuation of politics by other means," and that aphorism remains as true in the 21st century as it was in the 19th: The future of warfare will depend on geopolitics.[1] In this report, we focus on six key geopolitical trends that will shape who, how, where, when, and why the United States will fight in the next conflict (see Table S.1): U.S. polarization and retrenchment, China's rise, Asia's reassessment, the emergence of a revanchist Russia, upheaval in Europe, and turmoil in the Islamic world.

First, the United States emerged as one of the primary actors (perhaps *the* primary actor) on the world stage during a period of relative political unity about foreign policy matters—particularly about the need to contain communism and uphold liberal internationalism, which coupled U.S. military power with a belief in multilateral compromises. This consensus, however, has gradually eroded over the past several decades; today, Americans are becoming increasingly polarized and uncertain about the U.S. role in the world. The United States' retreat from its global position (whether because of political gridlock or policy choice) could affect everything from its defense budgets to its willingness to commit forces abroad.

Second, and at the same time, China is rising both economically and militarily. China, historically, has challenged even more-powerful adversaries to advance domestic priorities and to defend and expand its strategic periphery. In the future, as Chinese President Xi Jinping faces

[1] Carl von Clausewitz, *On War*, ed. and trans. Michael Howard and Peter Paret, Princeton, N.J.: Princeton University Press, 1984, p. 87.

Table S.1
Summary of Findings

Trend	Who Will Fight	How They Might Fight	Where They Might Fight	When They Might Fight	Why They Might Fight
U.S. polarization and retrenchment	United States	Airpower and special operations forces rather than conventional ground forces			Overconfidence in the military combined with distrust of other tools of national power
China's rise	China and its immediate neighbors	High-end conflict but also measures short of war	Taiwan, South China Sea, Senkaku Islands	If China's economy slows; potentially as President Xi Jinping's tenure comes to a close	Domestic pressure; expanding strategic periphery
Asia's reassessment	More new partners and allies (e.g., Vietnam/India); less others (e.g., the Philippines)	More maritime conflicts (air-sea cooperation)			Nationalism; fear of rising China
A revanchist Russia	Russia and its neighbors	High-end threat but also measures short of war	Russia's near abroad (with second-order effects for Asia and the Middle East)		Combination of Russian insecurity and desire for a greater sphere of influence
Upheaval in Europe	More Poland and France; less Germany; more-restrained United Kingdom		Eastern Europe (in response to Russian aggression)		Counterterrorism; Response to Russian aggression
Turmoil in the Islamic world	Terrorist groups, Arab States, Iran, Israel	Sustained low-level conflict/ counterterrorism	Middle East, North Africa, Central Asia	Now ongoing	Counterterrorism/ alliance entrapment

domestic pressure at home and as China's strategic periphery expands throughout the Indo-Pacific, it might be more likely to fight for those same reasons.

Third, as China rises, the rest of Asia faces a stark strategic choice: to balance or bandwagon with Beijing. The paths these countries choose will, in turn, have profound implications for the U.S. alliance architecture in the Indo-Pacific. Some states, such as India and Vietnam, will likely develop closer bonds with the United States, while other relationships—notably the Philippines and, perhaps, South Korea—will likely become more precarious.

Fourth, although China's rise threatens to upend the dynamic in Asia (and, perhaps, globally), the United States also confronts the reemergence of its old nemesis, Russia. After several decades of relative quiet after the Cold War, Russia has become increasingly aggressive, especially in its near abroad. Conceiving of itself as a leading international power, albeit a frustrated one, Russia has been increasingly willing to use military force—and coercion below the threshold of war—to block expansion of the North Atlantic Treaty Organization and the European Union into its near abroad, protect ethnic Russians and Russian speakers, and promote its interests as a great power.

Fifth, just as Russia has reemerged as a threat, Europe risks becoming increasingly fragmented and absorbed with its own challenges. Europe confronts a series of challenges—migration, terrorism, and populism, as well as a resurgent Russia—that threaten to undermine the European Union's ability to respond effectively to these threats, which could alter U.S. alliances.

Finally, although China and Russia arguably pose a greater strategic threat, U.S. wars since at least the terrorist attacks of September 11, 2001, have focused on three interconnected challenges emanating from the Islamic world—specifically, terrorism, weak states, and growing proxy wars. Looking ahead to 2030, these three challenges will likely continue to shape the future of warfare and drive U.S. military commitments.

Together, these six trends point to three overarching findings. First, many of the underlying geopolitical assumptions in the U.S.

National Defense Strategy[2]—about the centrality of great-power competition and the risk of aggression in the Indo-Pacific, Europe, and the Middle East—are correct. Second, although U.S. adversaries will likely remain relatively stable over the next decade, U.S. allies will likely change, especially as Europe becomes increasingly preoccupied with its own problems and Asia realigns as a result of the rise of China. Finally, and most importantly, U.S. strategists will face a deepening series of strategic dilemmas as the possibility of conflict in the Indo-Pacific, Europe, and the Middle East pull limited U.S. resources in different directions.

---

[2] U.S. Department of Defense, *Summary of the 2018 National Defense Strategy of the United States: Sharpening American Military's Competitive Edge*, Washington, D.C., January 2018.

Acknowledgments

This study would not have been possible without the help of many people. First and foremost, we thank Brig Gen David Hicks, Col Linc Bonner, and Scott Wheeler of the Air Force A5S for sponsoring this project and guiding it along the way. We would also like to thank Paula Thornhill, the Project AIR FORCE strategy doctrine program director, for her guidance and mentorship of this study. This report also benefited from the thoughtful reviews of Amb. James Dobbins and Hal Brands. Finally, the research team owes a special debt of gratitude to more than a hundred experts across the globe who volunteered their time to give their perspectives on the future of warfare both within their regions and globally. Human subjects protocol prevents us from thanking individuals by name, but we would like to thank the following institutions for hosting our research visits: United Kingdom (UK) Ministry of Defence's Development, Concepts, and Doctrine Centre; UK Parliament; Royal Institute of International Affairs (Chatham House); Control Risks; Royal United Services Institute for Defence and Security Studies; London School of Economics and Political Science IDEAS; International Institute of Strategic Studies; North Atlantic Treaty Organization Headquarters; European Commission; Centre for European Policy Studies; European Centre for International Political Economy; German Federal Ministry of Defence; German Institute for International and Security Affairs; German Federal Parliament; German Federal Foreign Office; European Council on Foreign Relations; Polish Ministry of Foreign Affairs; Polish Ministry of National Defence; Polish Institute of International Affairs; Centre for Eastern Studies; Interdisciplinary Center Herzliya; University of Jordan; Jordanian Army Forces; Royal Jordanian Air Force; Strategic Intelligence Solutions; Middle East Media and Policy Studies Institute–Centre for Strategic and International Studies; Strategic Intelligence Solutions; U.S. Embassy, Amman, Jordan; U.S. Embassy, Abu Dhabi, United Arab Emirates; Peking University Institute for International and Strategic Studies; Institute for China–U.S. People to People Exchange; Chinese Academy of Social Sciences; China Institute for Contemporary International Relations; University of International Relations; China Institute for International Studies; China Institute for International Strategic Studies; China Foundation for International Strategic Studies; Carnegie Endowment/Tsinghua University; Agence France Presse; *New York Times*; *Wall Street Journal*; *China Policy*; Japanese Ministry of Defense; Japanese Ministry of Foreign Affairs; Sasakawa Peace Foundation; and Hosei University.

Abbreviations

EU	European Union
GDP	gross domestic product
ISIS	Islamic States of Iraq and Syria
NATO	North Atlantic Treaty Organization
PLA	People's Liberation Army
UK	United Kingdom
USAF	U.S. Air Force
V4	the Visegrád Group (Hungary, Slovakia, Poland, and the Czech Republic)

CHAPTER ONE

Global Political Trends

Carl von Clausewitz famously argued that "war is the continuation of politics by other means," and that aphorism remains as true in the 21st century as it was in the 19th: The future of warfare will depend on geopolitics.[1] What that future looks like, however, remains far from clear. As the U.S. *National Defense Strategy* claims, "We are facing increased global disorder, characterized by decline in the long-standing rules-based international order—creating a security environment more complex and volatile than any we have experienced in recent memory."[2] Although this could very well be true, we need to unpack such terms as *increased global disorder* and *more complex and volatile* to understand what this characterization means for the future of warfare, particularly because a significant body of scholarly literature comes to the opposite conclusion. Many scholars note that conflict—particularly great-power interstate war—has been on the decline for decades.[3]

---

[1] Carl von Clausewitz, *On War*, ed. and trans. Michael Howard and Peter Paret, Princeton, N.J.: Princeton University Press, 1984, p. 87.

[2] U.S. Department of Defense, *Summary of the 2018 National Defense Strategy of the United States: Sharpening American Military's Competitive Edge*, Washington, D.C., January 2018, p. 1.

[3] For variations on this argument, see John Mueller, "War Has Almost Ceased to Exist: An Assessment," *Political Science Quarterly*, Vol. 124, No. 2, 2009; Steven Pinker, *The Better Angels of Our Nature: Why Violence Has Declined*, New York: Penguin Books, 2012; and Thomas S. Szayna, Angela O'Mahony, Jennifer Kavanagh, Stephen Watts, Bryan Frederick, Tova C. Norlen, and Phoenix Voorhies, *Conflict Trends and Conflict Drivers: An Empirical Assessment of Historical Conflict Patterns and Future Conflict Projections*, Santa Monica, Calif.: RAND Corporation, RR-1063-A, 2017.

Consequently, after briefly explaining this report's methodology, we focus on six key trends that stand to reshape geopolitics: U.S. polarization and retrenchment, China's rise, Asia's reassessment, the emergence of a revanchist Russia, upheaval in Europe, and turmoil in the Islamic world. Together, these six trends point to three overarching findings. First, many of the underlying geopolitical assumptions in the *National Defense Strategy*—particularly about the centrality of great-power competition and risk of conflict in the Indo-Pacific, Europe, and the Middle East—are correct. Second, although U.S. adversaries will remain relatively stable over the next decade, U.S. allies will change, especially as Europe becomes increasingly preoccupied with its own problems and Asia realigns as a result of the rise of China. Finally, and most importantly, U.S. strategists will face a deepening series of strategic dilemmas as the possibility of conflict in the Indo-Pacific, Europe, and the Middle East pulls limited U.S. resources in different directions. Ultimately, interstate great-power war might remain a rare phenomenon—especially when viewed in the grander sweep of human history—but, compared with the recent past, the United States might be entering a time that is more strategically precarious and geopolitically unstable.

Trend Selection and Methodology

To begin with the obvious, this report is not, nor does it claim to be, a comprehensive analysis of all future geopolitical trends. A myriad of local, regional, and international dynamics will shape how states interact on the global stage, and no single volume could hope to explore all of them. Rather, in consultation with the sponsor of this work, the United States Air Force (USAF), this report focuses on the six geopolitical trends that will be the most important to U.S. defense strategy over the next decade. Three of the trends focus on the foreign policy preferences of the hegemon (United States), its only plausible challenger (China), and its old archenemy (Russia). Especially given the *National Defense Strategy*'s focus on great-power competition and the general importance that these three countries play—and will continue to play—in shaping global affairs, these countries deserve individual attention.[4] In contrast, the other three trends look at regional dynamics where the *National Defense Strategy* argues that the joint force will need to be able to "deter aggression" in the future—specifically, the Indo-Pacific, Europe, and the Middle East.[5]

Of course, this selection comes with trade-offs. For reasons of time and resources, this report did not look at potential drivers of conflict in the Americas or in Africa, on the assumption that these areas would be either peaceful, subordinated to other great-power competitions (e.g., between the United States and China over natural resources), or peripheral to U.S. defense policy. Even Iran and North Korea, which are identified as likely adversaries in U.S. strategy, are discussed here only within the broader regional context, rather than with the same country-level focus given to Russia and China. Although some of these other regions are discussed in other recent work by the RAND Corporation and in the accompanying volumes in this series, this is one limitation of this work and implicitly, if inadvertently, reinforces the bias of current U.S. defense to focus on certain regions at the expense of others.[6]

Beyond the geographical constraints, this analysis focuses its discussion on political and foreign-policy trends. Of course, other factors will have second-order effects on future geopolitics. Many of them are explored in depth in the sister volumes of this series, which focus on cross-cutting, global military, economic, environmental, and legal trends.[7] Consequently, to avoid duplication across the series and to

---

4 Department of Defense, 2018, p. 1.

5 Department of Defense, 2018, p. 6.

6 For another complementary approach to looking at the future of competition, see Michael J. Mazarr, Jonathan Blake, Abigail Casey, Tim McDonald, Stephanie Pezard, and Michael Spirtas, *Understanding the Emerging Era of International Competition: Theoretical and Historical Perspectives*, Santa Monica, Calif.: RAND Corporation, RR-2726-AF, 2018.

7 The other volumes in this series are Raphael S. Cohen, Nathan Chandler, Shira Efron, Bryan Frederick, Eugeniu Han, Kurt Klein, Forrest E. Morgan, Ashley L. Rhoades, Howard J. Shatz, and Yuliya Shokh, *The Future of Warfare in 2030: Project Overview and Conclusions*, Santa Monica, Calif.: RAND Corporation, RR-2849/1-AF, 2020; Forrest E. Morgan and Raphael S. Cohen, *Military Trends and the Future of Warfare: The Changing Global Environ-*

keep this volume shorter and more accessible, they are discussed here only in passing.

To study the political and foreign-policy trends, we relied on three sources of information: official policy announcements and documents, other scholarly work, and an extensive set of interviews. Over the course of the project, the research team interviewed more than 120 different government, military, academic, and policy experts from more than 50 different institutions in Belgium, China, Germany, Israel, Japan, Jordan, Poland, the United Arab Emirates, and the United Kingdom (UK) for their perspectives on regional and global trends that might shape the future of conflict between now and 2030.

For the most part in this volume, we assume linear projections in each of the trends while noting what events could derail such projections. In practice, the future of warfare will be determined by the interaction of several trends in different areas. Analysis of this interaction can be found in the summary volume of the series, but before this aggregation can be done, we need to parse the individual components, starting with the six geopolitical trends presented in this volume.[8]

---

ment and Its Implications for the U.S. Air Force, Santa Monica, Calif.: RAND Corporation, RR-2849/3-AF, 2020; Howard J. Shatz and Nathan Chandler, *Global Economic Trends and the Future of Warfare: The Changing Global Environment and Its Implications for the U.S. Air Force*, Santa Monica, Calif.: RAND Corporation, RR-2849/4-AF, 2020; Shira Efron, Kurt Klein, and Raphael S. Cohen, *Environment, Geography, and the Future of Warfare: The Changing Global Environment and Its Implications for the U.S. Air Force*, Santa Monica, Calif.: RAND Corporation, RR-2849/5-AF, 2020; and Bryan Frederick and Nathan Chandler, *Restraint and the Future of Warfare: The Changing Global Environment and Its Implications for the U.S. Air Force*, Santa Monica, Calif.: RAND Corporation, RR-2849/6-AF, 2020.

[8] See Cohen et al., 2020.

CHAPTER TWO

Trend 1: U.S. Polarization and Retrenchment

In the spring of 1948, the Republican chairman of the Senate Foreign Relations Committee and presidential candidate, Arthur Vandenberg, crossed party lines to work with the man he sought to unseat in the White House, President Harry S. Truman, to pass the so-called Vandenberg Resolution. The resolution did little to help Vandenberg's presidential prospects, but it profoundly shaped future of U.S. foreign policy.[1] It affirmed the concept of collective defense, paving the way for the North Atlantic Treaty Organization (NATO) and cementing the role of the United States as a global security provider.[2] Vandenberg's actions underscored his most notable line: "We must stop politics at the water's edge."[3] Today, Americans are shifting away from Vandenberg in both sentiment and substance and becoming increasingly polarized and uncertain about the role of the United States in the world. Whether because of political gridlock or policy choice, if the United States backs away from its global position, there will be profound effects on the future of warfare.

Context: U.S. Centrality in Geopolitics

Emerging as the strongest great power after World War II, the United States crafted the institutions and norms that define the international

---

[1] U.S. Senate, Resolution 239, 90th Congress, 2nd session, June 11, 1948.

[2] Greg Myre, "Taking U.S. Politics Beyond 'The Water's Edge,'" NPR, March 10, 2015.

[3] Myre, 2015.

order. After the Soviet Union's collapse and the dawning of the "unipolar moment," it also became the de facto enforcer of that order and served, if somewhat unwillingly, as the "global policeman."[4] Although some scholars question whether these actions have contributed to or detracted from world peace, few doubt the centrality of the U.S. role in shaping world events.[5] As a result, if the United States chooses to retreat from its role of global superpower, it will have far-reaching consequences.

Historical Trend: Increasing U.S. Polarization of Foreign Policy

For the two and a half centuries that the United States has existed, Americans have never been wholly of one mind about any policy issue, and the nation has gone through cycles of political unity and division. Still, it has emerged as one of the primary actors—perhaps the primary actor—on the world stage during a period of relative political unity that has gradually eroded over the past several decades.

During the Second World War, partisanship ebbed. In 1950, the American Political Science Association published a report, *Toward a More Responsible Two-Party System*, bemoaning the lack of clear ideological cleavages. It argued that "popular government in a nation of more than 150 million people requires political parties which provide the electorate with a proper range of choice between alternatives of action."[6] Similarly, University of California, Berkeley, political scientist Herbert McClosky found that, compared with the overall population, "influentials" (defined as those who attended the 1956 presiden-

---

[4] Charles Krauthammer, "The Unipolar Moment," *Foreign Affairs*, Vol. 70, No. 1, 1990/1991.

[5] Perhaps, the dominant view is that U.S. hegemony has helped maintain relative peace in the post–Cold War period. See Stephen G. Brooks and William C. Wohlforth, *World Out of Balance: International Relations and the Challenge of American Primacy*, Princeton, N.J.: Princeton University Press, 2008. For the counterargument that U.S. hegemony has, in fact, led to a more violent world, see Nuno P. Monteiro, "Unrest Assured: Why Unipolarity Is Not Peaceful," *International Security*, Vol. 36, No. 3, Winter 2011/2012.

[6] Committee on Political Parties, *Toward a More Responsible Two-Party System*, Menesha, Wisc.: American Political Science Association, 1950, p. 15.

tial conventions) displayed "greater faith in the capacity of the mass of men to govern themselves . . . believe more firmly in political equality, and . . . more often disdain the 'extreme' beliefs embodied in the Right Wing, Left Wing, totalitarian, elitist, and authoritarian scales."[7] Finally, quantitative analyses show that roughly a quarter of U.S. Congressmen in the mid-20th century were centrists.[8]

Americans proved particularly united on foreign policy. Noting that between the Japanese attack on Pearl Harbor in 1941 and the Tet Offensive in Vietnam in 1968, roughly three-quarters of congressional foreign policy votes were taken on a bipartisan basis,[9] political scientists Charles Kupchan and Peter Trubowitz remark:

> To be sure, partisan politics did not always stop at the water's edge; Republicans and Democrats often clashed over foreign aid and trade matters. Partisan divisions, however, were sporadic and transitory. On the basic elements of grand strategy—when military force should be used, the importance of international support, and the role of multilateral institutions—consensus was the norm.[10]

Even during this period of relative unity, there were still vicious partisan debates over the Chinese civil war, McCarthyism, the Korean War, and other issues. Nonetheless, compared with other periods, there was a bipartisan consensus that favored liberal internationalism—coupling U.S. military power with belief in multilateral compromises.[11]

During the Vietnam War, this consensus began to break down.[12] Although most Americans still believed that communism needed to be

---

[7] Herbert McClosky, "Consensus and Ideology in American Politics," *American Political Science Review*, Vol. 58, No. 2, June 1964, p. 366.

[8] See Charles A. Kupchan and Peter L. Trubowitz, "Dead Center and the Demise of Liberal Internationalism," *International Security*, Vol. 32, No. 2, Fall 2007, p. 21, Figure 2.

[9] Kupchan and Trubowitz, 2007, p. 11.

[10] Kupchan and Trubowitz, 2007, p. 12.

[11] Kupchan and Trubowitz, 2007, p. 8.

[12] Admittedly, some scholars dispute this finding. See Stephen Chaudon, Helen V. Milner, and Dustin H. Tingley, "The Center Still Holds," *International Security*, Vol. 35, No. 1,

contained, many also believed that "the United States had fallen prey to errant leadership, exaggerated threats, and the excessive use of U.S. power."[13] Additionally, as conservative southern Democrats and liberal northern Republicans disappeared, ideological lines between the parties grew starker.[14] The disintegration of the unifying threat of the Soviet Union and the start of a series of wars of choice—first during the humanitarian interventions in the 1990s and particularly in Iraq in the 2000s—only exacerbated this divide.[15]

Foreign policy views mirrored broader trends in the U.S. electorate. Pew survey data indicate that median Republican and Democratic voters moved farther apart on a range of issues. More troubling, the divide grew starker among voters who were more politically engaged (Figure 2.1).[16]

Political polarization extends to such issues as defense spending.[17] In 2017, a full 62 percent of Republicans believed the United States spent too little on defense, compared with 34 percent of independents and 15 percent of Democrats.[18] And the partisan gap is growing. In 2012, there was only a 32-percent difference between Republicans and

Summer 2010. That said, the weight of scholarly opinion is on the other side. See Kupchan and Trubowitz, 2007; Charles A. Kupchan and Peter L. Trubowitz, "The Illusion of Liberal Internationalism's Revival," *International Security*, Vol. 35, No. 1, Summer 2010; and Gyung-Ho Jeong and Paul J. Quirk, "Division at the Water's Edge: The Polarization of Foreign Policy," *American Politics Research*, July 2017.

[13] Kupchan and Trubowitz, 2007, p. 22.

[14] Kupchan and Trubowitz, 2007, pp. 31–39; Jeong and Quirk, 2017, p. 25.

[15] Kupchan and Trubowitz, 2007, pp. 27–31; Jeong and Quirk, 2017, p. 25.

[16] For an alternate finding, see Morris P. Fiorina and Samuel J. Abrams, "Political Polarization in the American Public," *Annual Review of Political Science*, Vol. 11, 2008. Importantly, while Fiorina and Abrams doubt mass polarization, they still acknowledge and accept that U.S. elites have polarized.

[17] For earlier historical data confirming this same trend, see Kupchan and Trubowitz, 2007, p. 38, Figure 6.

[18] Art Swift, "1 in 3 Americans Say U.S. Spends Too Little on Defense," Gallup, March 2, 2017.

Figure 2.1
Growing Polarization of the U.S. Electorate

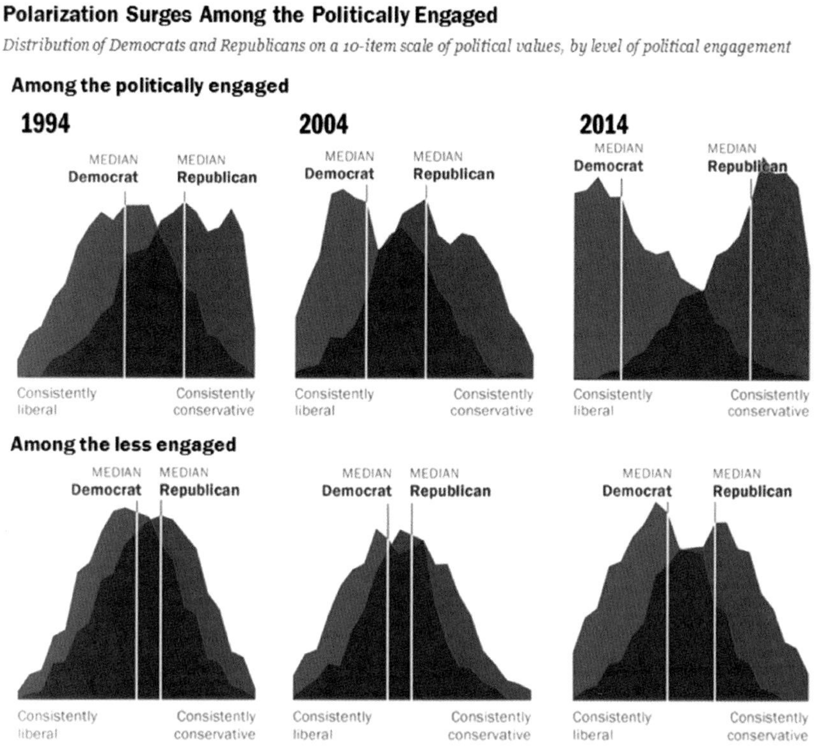

NOTES: Ideological consistency based on a scale of 10 political values questions. Republicans include Republican-leaning independents; Democrats include Democratic-leaning independents. Politically engaged are defined as those who are registered to vote, follow government and public affairs most of the time, and say they vote always or nearly always.
SOURCE: "Political Polarization in the American Public," webpage, Pew Research Center, June 12, 2014.

Democrats on this issue, compared with the 47-percent gap today.[19] Unsurprisingly, the Defense Department's budget is increasingly caught up in the broader partisan battles over the national budget.

[19] In 2012, 42 percent of Republicans, 22 percent of independents, and 10 percent of Democrats thought that the United States spent too little on defense. Swift, 2017.

At the same time, Americans are increasingly divided about enforcing international order. Because war resolutions are unpopular, Congress has not officially declared war since the Second World War. Although lawmakers authorized the use of military against those connected to the September 11, 2001, terrorist attacks and to "prevent any future acts of international terrorism," they have avoided passing another authorization since—despite new engagements in Libya against the Moammar Qaddafi regime and later against the Islamic State in Iraq and Syria (ISIS)—partly because there was no consensus about what such an authorization should contain.[20] Similarly, although Congress authorized the Iraq War in 2003, lawmakers proved unable to curtail that conflict as that war became increasingly unpopular.

Polling similarly suggests that Americans are increasingly dubious about using force—especially ground troops—to enforce the international order. For example, even well into the Libya campaign in 2011, Americans were evenly split about the intervention in Libya and overwhelmingly (61 percent) disagreed (38 percent of them strongly) with sending in ground troops.[21] In 2017, some 57 percent of Americans approved when the Trump administration launched a series of punitive strikes in Syria against Bashar Assad's regime in retaliation for its use of chemical weapons, but a mere 18 percent were willing to commit ground troops to the task.[22] Most recently, as nuclear tensions on the Korean Peninsula rose, only half of Americans backed military action against the regime and about a third supported sending ground troops.[23]

---

[20] Public Law 107-40, Authorization for Use of Military Force Against Terrorists, September 18, 2001.

[21] YouGov, "61% Oppose Sending U.S. Ground Troops to Libya," Economist/YouGov Poll, June 10, 2011.

[22] Jennifer De Pinto, Fred Backus, Kabir Khanna, and Anthony Salvanto, "What Americans Think About U.S. Strike on Syria," CBS News, April 10, 2017.

[23] Steven Shepard, "Poll: No Increase in Support for Military Action in North Korea," *Politico*, August 16, 2017.

Future Projection: Gridlock, Disillusionment, and Isolationism

Unfortunately, there is little reason to believe that the growing polarization of the U.S. electorate will reverse any time soon. On a structural level, despite the periodic calls for a third party, the two major parties will continue to hold power. Since the mid-19th century, the presidency has always been occupied by either a Republican or Democrat, and although independents have done better at state and local levels, they still make up only a small minority of office-holders. On a substantive level, the geographic, socioeconomic, racial, and cultural cleavages driving polarization—coastal versus heartland, blue-collar versus white-collar, minority race versus white—do not seem any closer to resolution.

Two predictions follow from this trend. First, barring a cataclysmic event (e.g., another September 11 terrorist attack), partisan gridlock will likely continue. This, in turn, will limit political leaders' ability to push major new initiatives through Congress—including those related to foreign and defense policy.

Second, U.S. disillusionment with global engagement could continue to grow. In Gallup polling, the percentage of Americans expressing "very little" or "no" faith in the presidency and Congress has increased dramatically since 2002 (Figure 2.2). Indeed, the only U.S. governmental institution in which most Americans consistently express a "great deal" or "quite a lot" of confidence is the military—since 2001, the military has consistently polled above 70 percent.[24] If these trends continue, future policymakers might more readily turn to military solutions.

As for whether Americans will back away from liberal internationalism, the trend is somewhat more ambiguous. Gallup polling dating back to the turn of the millennium suggests that Americans are increasingly dissatisfied with their role in the world order (Figure 2.3). Similarly, a 2016 Pew survey found that 57 percent of Americans believed that the United States should "deal with its own problems and let other

[24] Gallup, undated-a.

Figure 2.2
Percentage of Americans Expressing "Very Little" or "No" Faith in Government Institutions

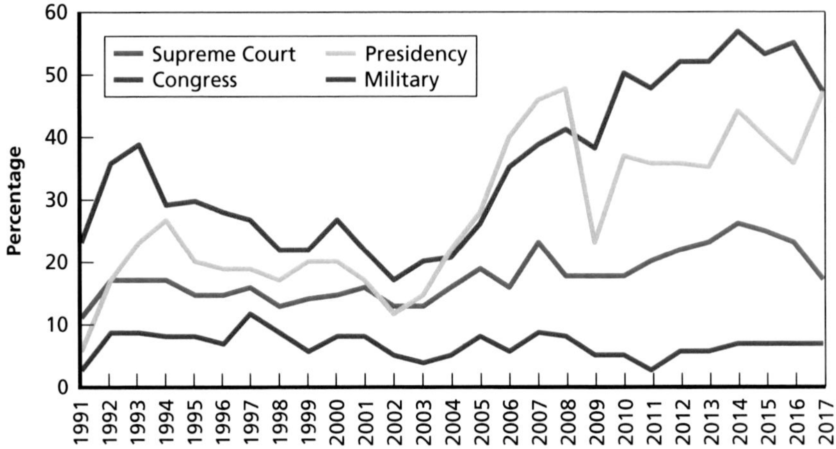

SOURCE: Gallup, "Confidence in Institutions," webpage, undated-a.

countries deal with their own problems as best they can."[25] Previous surveys similarly suggested that Americans increasingly believe that the United States should "mind its own business" and "should not think so much in international terms but concentrate more on our own national problems and building up our strength and prosperity here at home."[26]

These sentiments, however, have not always translated into U.S. foreign policy. President Barack Obama promised "that [it is] time to focus on nation building here at home," but he still ordered a troop surge in Afghanistan and a military intervention in Libya.[27] Likewise, President Donald Trump promised an "America first" strategy, but less

[25] Bruce Drake and Carroll Doherty, "Key Findings on How Americans View the U.S. Role in the World," Washington, D.C., Pew Research Center, May 5, 2016.

[26] "Public Sees U.S. Power Declining as Support for Global Engagement Slips," webpage, Pew Research Center, December 3, 2013.

[27] Katelyn Sabochik, "President Obama on the Way Forward in Afghanistan," Obama White House Archives, June 22, 2011.

Figure 2.3
Percentage of Americans Expressing Satisfaction with U.S. Role in the World

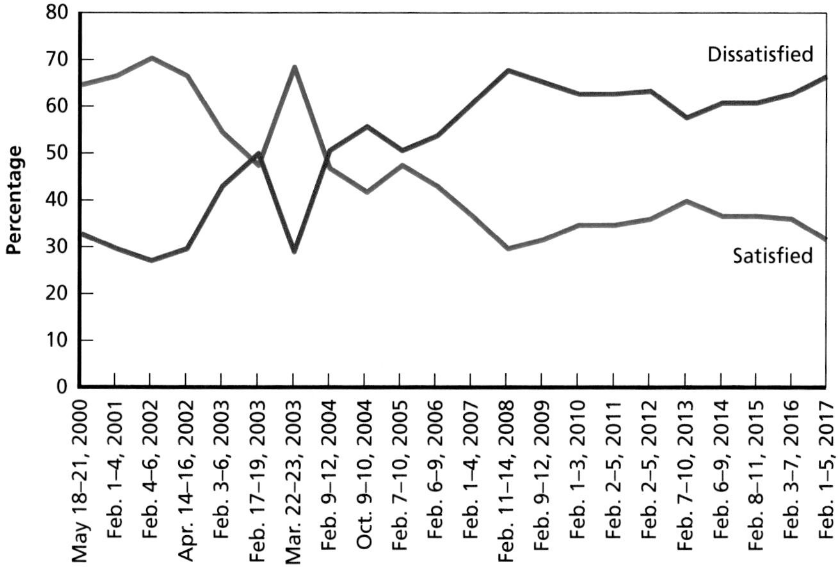

SOURCE: Gallup, "U.S. Position in the World," webpage, undated-b.

than three months after taking office, he ordered airstrikes against the Assad regime for using chemical weapons, both for humanitarian reasons and to uphold the Chemical Weapons Convention and United Nations Security Council resolutions.[28]

Whether future leaders will continue to buck popular sentiment remains an open question. As political leaders of the Cold War generation gradually retire from public life, there might be fewer vocal advocates for U.S. internationalism. A study by the libertarian Cato Institute suggests that the millennial generation sees the world as less threatening, is more skeptical about military intervention, and is more

[28] Donald J. Trump, "Inaugural Address," White House website, January 2017a. For Trump's justification of the airstrikes, see Donald J. Trump, "Full Transcript: Trump Statement on Syria Strikes," via *Politico*, April 6, 2017b.

likely to support "a more restrained grand strategy."[29] Moreover, as the United States faces budgetary pressure with mounting deficits, growing entitlement obligations, and competing domestic spending priorities, the political pressure to avoid costly foreign interventions will likely grow.

Implications for the U.S. Air Force and the Future of Warfare

America's growing polarization, disillusionment, and isolationism will probably have at least three major effects on the future of warfare. First, partisan gridlock and disillusionment preventing the United States from acting as a global superpower could create a power vacuum, allowing other powers (particularly China and Russia) to try to fill the void.

Second, and more specifically, U.S. political dynamics could make the USAF an increasingly attractive policy tool. Some scholars also suggest that, in a polarized environment, politicians might use force to galvanize their base.[30] In this case, though, the overhang of the Iraq and Afghanistan wars could limit Americans' appetite for use of conventional ground troops. The net effect of these countervailing trends might then push policymakers to employ the less politically risky options of air power and special operations forces whenever possible.

Third, these trends within U.S. society could affect military recruiting, although it is less clear to what effect. On the one hand, Americans becoming more disillusioned with overseas military commitments and more broadly unsure about the role of the United States in the world could dampen recruiting efforts. On the other hand, enlistment decisions are also based on economic and personal variables,

---

[29] A. Trevor Thrall and Erik Goepner, *Millennials and U.S. Foreign Policy: The Next Generation's Attitudes Towards Foreign Policy and War (and Why They Matter)*, Washington, D.C.: Cato Institute, 2017, p. 1.

[30] See Jack Snyder, Robert Y. Shapiro, and Yaeli Bloch-Elkon, "Free Hand Abroad, Divide and Rule at Home," *World Politics*, Vol. 61, No. 1, January 2009.

and, given that the military as an institution remains popular, there might not be much of a net effect.

Finally, congressional gridlock might affect what tools are available to the USAF to fight future wars. Because "the troops" remain uniformly popular even if the wars they fight are not, Congress will continue to spend on pay and benefits for military personnel. Even during the recent budget battles, uniformed personnel were largely spared the pay freezes and government shutdowns affecting the other parts of the federal government. Instead, the Department of Defense's procurement and readiness accounts likely will take center stage in the budget battles over the next decade or so. Because the USAF depends as a service on advanced technology and high-end weapon systems for its lifeblood, continued partisan gridlock could reduce the USAF's competitive edge, particularly over near-peer adversaries.

CHAPTER THREE

Trend 2: China's Rise

The United States remains mired in its own problems, but the rest of the world is not standing still. As the 2017 National Security Strategy argues, China is "seeking to displace the United States in the Indo-Pacific region, expand the reaches of its state-driven economic model, and reorder the region in its favor."[1] Historically, China has challenged adversaries that were even more powerful than the United States is now to advance China's domestic priorities and to defend and expand its strategic periphery. In the future, as Chinese President Xi Jinping faces domestic pressure at home and as China's strategic periphery expands throughout the Indo-Pacific, China might be more likely to fight for those same reasons.

Context: China's Priorities Include Growing Military Ambition

According to its diplomatic statements, China's security interests are mostly focused on domestic issues—maintaining the stability of the political system and the Communist party rule, promoting economic development, and preserving its sovereignty and territorial integrity.[2] China also seeks to pacify resistant populations in Xinjiang and Tibet,

---

[1] Executive Office of the President, *National Security Strategy*, Washington, D.C., 2017, p. 25.

[2] Chinese leaders often emphasize "national sovereignty, national security, and (economic) development" [维护国家主权、安全、发展利益] as top interests. See, for example, "Xi Jin-

regain control over Taiwan, and assert its maritime claims in the East and South China Seas.[3]

Chinese military documents, however, take a more expansive view of Chinese security. The 2013 Defense White Paper states that China should build a "strong national defense and powerful armed forces which are commensurate with China's international standing."[4] The 2015 Defense White Paper, similarly, argues that "for the foreseeable future a world war is unlikely," but recognizes that China has "important strategic opportunity" to realize the "great national rejuvenation."[5] The paper calls for the development of a global military power capable of "protecting distant sea lanes" and emphasizes "preparation for military struggle," as well as building an ability to "fight and win wars" and uphold the rule of the Chinese Communist Party.[6]

More troubling, the "great rejuvenation of the Chinese nation"—Xi's signature notion—requires building a strong military "now more than any time in history."[7] Xi's vision of the future focuses on returning China to the predominance in Asia that it enjoyed prior to Western intrusion; reestablishing control over "Greater China," including Xinjiang, Tibet, Hong Kong, and Taiwan; recovering its historical sphere

---

ping Attends PLA Delegation Plenary Meeting" ["习近平出席解放军代表团全体会议"], *People's Daily* [人民日报], March 11, 2014.

3 Embassy of the People's Republic of China in the United States of America, "国防部：大陆对台湾军事部署是否调整将视情况而定" ["Ministry of Defense: Adjustments to Mainland Military Disposition Toward Taiwan Will Depend on the Situation"], Washington, D.C., 2008.

4 State Council Information Office, *The Diversified Employment of China's Armed Forces*, Beijing, April 2013.

5 State Council Information Office, *China's Military Strategy*, Beijing, May 2015, pp. 4–9.

6 In his speech at the 90th anniversary of the People's Liberation Army (PLA), Xi Jinping said: "The most important thing, I think, is that when the party and the people need it, can our army always adhere to the absolute leadership of the party, is it able to start and win a war . . . ?" Ministry of National Defense of the People's Republic of China, "胜战之问" ["The Issue of Successful War"], August 2, 2017.

7 "China Focus: 'Be Ready to Win Wars,' China's Xi Orders Reshaped PLA," Xinhua News, August 1, 2017.

of influence along its borders, as well as in the adjacent seas; and commanding the respect of other great powers.[8]

Historical Trend: Not So Peaceful

Despite China's official emphasis on "peaceful development,"[9] modern China has never been entirely peaceful.[10] Chinese leaders historically used force to preempt a direct attack or encroachment of Chinese territory, recover lost territories, and enhance its regional and global stature.[11] Although Beijing claims that force was a measure of last resort, China repeatedly used force to protect its sphere of influence and support its domestic political aims—even against more-powerful adversaries.[12]

China's first and most significant large-scale military intervention occurred during the Korean War (1950–1953), shortly after the foundation of communist China in 1949.[13] Mao Zedong worried that

---

[8] Graham Allison, *Destined for War: Can America and China Escape Thucydides's Trap?* Boston: Houghton Mifflin Harcourt, 2017.

[9] State Council Information Office, "China's Peaceful Development," Beijing, government white paper, 2011.

[10] For a discussion of China's traditional politics of power, see Yuan-Kang Wang, *Harmony and War: Confucian Culture and Chinese Power Politics*, New York: Columbia University Press, 2010. After reviewing Chinese military history over the past six centuries, Wang concludes that, despite the dominance of the antimilitarist Confucian culture, China has regularly practiced realpolitik and expansive grand strategies.

[11] John W. Garver, *Foreign Relations of the People's Republic of China*, Vol. 9, Englewood Cliffs, N.J.: Prentice Hall, 1993, pp. 253–254. Also see Michael D. Swaine, Sara A. Daly, and Peter W. Greenwood, *Interpreting China's Grand Strategy: Past, Present, and Future*, Santa Monica, Calif.: RAND Corporation, MR-1121-AF, 2000, p. 21.

[12] Andrew Scobell, *China's Use of Military Force: Beyond the Great Wall and the Long March*, New York: Cambridge University Press, 2003, p. 193.

[13] For a detailed account of China's participation in the Korean War, see Allen Suess Whiting, *China Crosses the Yalu: The Decision to Enter the Korean War*, Palo Alto, Calif.: Stanford University Press, 1968; Hao Yufan and Zhai Zhihai, "China's Decision to Enter the Korean War: History Revisited," *China Quarterly*, Vol. 121, 1990; Chen Jian, *China's Road to the Korean War: The Making of the Sino-American Confrontation*, New York: Columbia

the communist revolution was losing momentum and needed external threats to consolidate his position at home.[14] Beijing was also alarmed by a U.S. rapid advance toward the border with China and feared that U.S. troops could be permanently stationed in North Korea.[15] China was also disturbed by U.S. Seventh Fleet movement into the Taiwan Strait and continuing U.S. support of the Kuomintang regime.[16] Whatever the true motivation, China entered into a war against a stronger, nuclear-capable adversary, despite being relatively unprepared and unsure about Soviet aid.[17] China deployed more than 2.3 million troops—including more than 66 percent of the entire field army, all its tank divisions, and more than 70 percent of its air force, suffering total casualties of 360,000.[18] Nevertheless, Mao considered the Korean War a success.[19]

Although Mao postponed his promise to "liberate" Taiwan after the beginning of the Korean War, China never abandoned that goal of reunification and used force to prevent that goal from slipping away. In 1953, the United States increased fighter aircraft deliveries, signed the Agreement on Mutual Military Understanding, and discussed a possible formal alliance with Taiwan. In response, the PLA shelled the Kuomintang-controlled Jinmen island in September 1954 during the First Taiwan Strait Crisis.[20] A few years later, during the Second

---

University Press, 1995b; and William Stueck, *The Korean War: An International History*, Princeton, N.J.: Princeton University Press, 1997. This discussion of China's intervention mainly relies on Jian's account; his work is largely based on verifiable Chinese sources, but it is important to recognize that there is no academic consensus about Mao's motives.

[14] Jian, 1995b, pp. 213–215.

[15] Thomas J. Christensen, "Windows and War: Trend Analysis and Beijing's Use of Force," in Alastair Iain Johnston and Robert S. Ross, eds., *New Directions in the Study of China's Foreign Policy*, Palo Alto, Calif.: Stanford University Press, 2006.

[16] Jian, 1995b, p. 216.

[17] Jian, 1995b, pp. 199–200.

[18] Yufan and Zhihai, 1990, p. 114.

[19] Jian, 1995b, pp. 220–222.

[20] M. Taylor Fravel, "Power Shifts and Escalation: Explaining China's Use of Force in Territorial Disputes," *International Security*, Vol. 32, No. 3, 2008.

Taiwan Strait Crisis in 1958, the PLA shelled the Kinmen (Quemoy) and Matsu islands in response to the November 1957 U.S.-Taiwanese joint military exercises and the creation of the U.S.-Taiwan Defense Command in March 1958; the bombing additionally served to deter a potential U.S. commitment to defend Kinmen and other coastal islands.[21] Mao also saw the shelling as a chance to send a larger message to the West and to the Soviet Union about China's independence and to consolidate support at home.[22] Importantly, both the First and Second Taiwan Strait Crises were intentionally limited uses of force to send political messages.[23]

During the Vietnam War (1964–1969), Mao wanted to drive the United States out of Vietnam, compete with the Soviet Union for global influence, and still avoid a direct war with the United States.[24] As a result, China sent significant amounts of military and civilian aid, engineering troops to build and maintain defense works and railways, and anti-aircraft artillery troops to protect critical strategic assets in North Vietnam.[25] China's military forces reached 170,000 at one point during 1967–1968.[26]

Simultaneously, the relationship between China and the Soviet Union deteriorated. The Soviet Union signed a pact with Outer Mongolia in 1967 and gradually increased its forces there to between eight

---

[21] Fravel, 2008, p. 62.

[22] Mao quoted in Wu Lengxi, "Inside Story of the Decision Making During the Shelling of Jinmen," *Zhuanji wenxue [Biographical Literature]*, No. 1, 1994, p. 11; Henry Kissinger and Nicholas Hormann, *On China*, New York: Penguin Press, 2011, p. 173.

[23] During the Second Taiwan Strait Crisis, Mao's field commander, Ye Fei, reported that Mao never gave orders to prepare for seizing the islands. Chinese military leader Lin Biao even entertained the idea of warning the United States in advance to ensure that no U.S. advisers got hurt, and Mao restricted air activity to avoid engaging U.S. aircraft. Cited in Christensen, 2006, pp. 62–63.

[24] Christensen, 2006, pp. 66–68.

[25] Chen Jian, "China's Involvement in the Vietnam War, 1964–69," *China Quarterly*, Vol. 142, 1995a.

[26] Christensen, 2006, p. 66.

and ten divisions by 1969.[27] Mao decided to use force to deter further Soviet advances.[28] Chinese forces attacked a Soviet outpost on Zhenbao (or Damanski) Island on March 2, 1969, killing several dozen soldiers and setting the stage for a larger battle two weeks later. Military action was accompanied by large-scale demonstrations against the Soviet Union involving, according to Beijing's claims, more than 400 million people.[29] Mao planned to shock the Soviet leadership into backing down in accordance with China's "offensive deterrence" strategy.[30] Instead, the war ended inconclusively, ultimately getting resolved in negotiations several decades later.

After two decades of calm following the opening up of China, a visit of the Taiwanese president Lee Teng-hui to the United States in June 1995 triggered the Third Taiwan Strait Crisis.[31] Fearing a Taiwanese declaration of independence, China launched six short-range ballistic tactical missiles targeting an area 90 miles away from Taiwan and conducted several live-fire tests in the coastal area of Fujian in July and August 1995. A few months later, China fired missiles less than 50 miles away from Taiwan's busiest ports. At the same time, China also tried to avoid escalation. All military exercises were defined in terms of duration, location, and scope, and were communicated in advance to Taipei and Washington to minimize the risk of a direct confrontation.[32] After the crisis, Beijing introduced new language in its 2000 White Paper on Taiwan, stating that China could resort to force

---

[27] Thomas W. Robinson, "The Sino-Soviet Border Dispute: Background, Development, and the March 1969 Clashes," *American Political Science Review*, Vol. 66, No. 4, 1972.

[28] William Burr, "Sino-American Relations, 1969: The Sino-Soviet Border War and Steps Towards Rapprochement," *Cold War History*, Vol. 1, No. 3, 2001.

[29] Robinson, 1972, p. 1201.

[30] Kissinger and Hormann, 2011, p. 217.

[31] For a detailed discussion of the Third Taiwan Strait Crisis, see Robert S. Ross, "The 1995–96 Taiwan Strait Confrontation: Coercion, Credibility, and the Use of Force," *International Security*, Vol. 25, No. 2, 2000; and Scobell, 2003, pp. 171–191.

[32] Scobell, 2003, pp. 176–177.

if Taipei authorities "refuse . . . the peaceful settlement of cross-Straits reunification through negotiations."[33]

Today, China contests its maritime borders in the East and South China Seas and its land border with India. These disputes have occasionally led to direct military conflict, such as the Chinese attack on Vietnamese forces near the Paracel Islands in 1974 and Fiery Cross Reef in 1988 and China's military ouster of Philippine forces from Mischief Reef in 1995.[34] More often, China has relied on measures short of war, such as economic coercion,[35] building on and militarizing islands in the South China Sea,[36] increasing its long-range bomber flights,[37] introducing air-defense identification zones,[38] and using its coast guard and maritime militia to coerce its regional neighbors.[39] These actions increase China's de facto control over regional waters and occasionally result in aircraft and naval incidents involving U.S. forces.[40]

In the past several years, modern China has used force less frequently than some other great powers, including the United States. That said, modern China has not been entirely peaceful either and has used force even against more-powerful adversaries—albeit usually in limited ways—to assert control over its strategic periphery and to con-

---

[33] State Council Information Office, "The One-China Principle and the Taiwan Issue," Beijing, government white paper, 2000.

[34] Peter Dutton, "Three Disputes and Three Objectives—China and the South China Sea," *Naval War College Review*, Vol. 64, No. 4, 2011.

[35] Dan Blumenthal, "Economic Coercion as a Tool in China's Grand Strategy," statement before the Senate Committee on Foreign Relations, July 24, 2018.

[36] For a list of recent incidents, see Ronald O'Rourke, *China's Actions in South and East China Seas: Implications for U.S. Interests—Background and Issues for Congress*, Washington, D.C.: Congressional Research Service, R42784, August 1, 2018, pp. 9–11.

[37] Mark R. Cozad and Nathan Beauchamp-Mustafaga, *People's Liberation Army Air Force Operations over Water: Maintaining Relevance in China's Changing Security Environment*, Santa Monica, Calif.: RAND Corporation, RR-2057-AF, 2017.

[38] Ian E. Rinehart and Bart Elias, *China's Air Defense Identification Zone (ADIZ)*, Washington, D.C.: Congressional Research Service, R43894, January 30, 2015.

[39] U.S. Department of Defense, *Annual Report to Congress, Military and Security Developments Involving the People's Republic of China*, Washington, D.C., 2017, p. 56.

[40] O'Rourke, 2018, pp. 12–15.

solidate domestic objectives. Consequently, a far stronger China might be even more likely to use force for similar reasons in the future.

Future Projection: Increasing Domestic Pressure; Expanding Strategic Periphery

By 2030, China could become increasingly willing to use force. Domestically, Xi has consolidated his power and lifted the presidential term limits, allowing him to remain in power indefinitely.[41] The formal shift in power also comes with a change in elite attitudes. Although measuring public opinion in China remains difficult, Chinese government officials we interviewed often spoke about Xi in glowing, if idolizing, terms, placing him on a pedestal next to Mao Zedong.[42]

This adoration of and centralization of power around Xi has several implications for China's willingness to use force. First, Xi has tightened his grip over the PLA, once thought be to growing independent of the party, possibly eliminating some of the checks on China's use of force.[43] Of perhaps more concern, as Chinese expectations for Xi's performance rise, so does the bar for Xi's success, meaning he might feel pressured to wage a "diversionary" conflict if the Chinese economy slows and the regime cannot justify its legitimacy-based economic growth.[44] There is a sense that the Chinese economy is slowing,

[41] Elizabeth C. Economy, "China's New Revolution: The Reign of Xi Jinping," *Foreign Affairs*, Vol. 97, No. 3, May–June 2018, p. 60.

[42] Interviews with multiple Chinese government-affiliated think tanks, Beijing, June 12–15, 2018.

[43] Joel Wuthnow and Phillip Charles Saunders, *Chinese Military Reform in the Age of Xi Jinping: Drivers, Challenges, and Implications*, Washington, D.C.: National Defense University Press, 2017; Scobell, 2003, p. 195.

[44] Erin Baggott Carter argues that when elite support declines because of economic shocks, the autocrat can inoculate himself against elite leadership challenges by courting popular support through diversionary aggression. Erin Baggott Carter, *Elite Welfare Shocks and Diversionary Foreign Policy: Evidence from China*, Los Angeles: University of Southern California, 2017.

although by how much is hard to tell.[45] As one Chinese think tank official warned, outsiders often underestimate the economic pressure on the regime.[46]

Simultaneously, China is advancing its claims in the East and South China seas. In recent years, Beijing built numerous military installations on artificial islands (including jamming equipment and ballistic missiles on the Spratly Islands) and airfields capable of receiving long-range bombers.[47] These bases could eventually enable China to declare an air defense identification zone similar to what China attempted in the East China Sea in 2014.[48] Similarly, China increased patrols by military aircraft and by coast guard and "civilian" fishing ships in the close proximity of Japanese territorial waters near the disputed Senkaku Islands in the East China Sea; these patrols will probably continue.[49]

Outside of the maritime domain, China's Belt and Road Initiative incorporates more than 60 countries and, in time, could increase China's global military presence. China already established a military base in Djibouti, and China might be considering a second facility in the Southern Pacific.[50] China's massive investments in port facilities

---

45 Interview with journalist, Beijing, June 16, 2018.

46 Interview with Chinese think tank official, Beijing, June 12, 2018.

47 U.S.–China Economic and Security Review Commission, "Annual Reports," webpage, undated; Michael Gordon and Jeremy Page, "China Installed Military Jamming Equipment on Spratly Islands, U.S. Says," *Wall Street Journal*, April 9, 2018; Reuters, "China Deploys Cruise Missiles on South China Sea Outposts—Reports," *The Guardian*, May 3, 2018; Bethlehem Feleke, "China Tests Bombers on South China Sea Island," CNN, May 21, 2018. For a year-by-year review of Chinese military developments, see the U.S.–China Economic and Security Review Commission annual reports from 2002 on.

48 O'Rourke, 2018, p. 2.

49 Japan scrambled a record number of fighter jets—1,168—between March 2016 and March 2017, with 851 incidents prompted by Chinese aircraft. Robert Harding, "Japan Scrambles Record Number of Jets as Tensions Rise with China," *Financial Times*, April 13, 2017; interview with senior Japanese Ministry of Defense official, Tokyo, June 18, 2018.

50 John Fei, "China's Overseas Military Base in Djibouti: Features, Motivations, and Policy Implications," *China Brief*, Vol. 17, No. 17, December 22, 2017; "China Is Reportedly Proposing a Permanent Military Base in the South Pacific," CNBC.com, April 9, 2018.

could pave the way for other overseas naval facilities, extending China's global reach.[51] Although not an immediate threat to the United States, Chinese expansion in the relative vicinity of U.S. military bases could produce additional tensions.[52]

Above all, Taiwan will remain one of the most plausible locations for an armed conflict. Chinese officials regard Taiwan as their foremost geopolitical objective.[53] Indeed, Xi sees "China's full reunification as essential to realizing national rejuvenation," and "resolving the Taiwan question" remains a key element of China's long-term strategy.[54] Consequently, Xi might view resolving the Taiwan issue before he leaves office as central to his legacy. And the repeated Taiwan Strait Crises show how a Taiwan crisis could lead to war.

In general, China will probably be careful about challenging the United States. As political scientist Graham Allison writes, "Chinese are strategically patient: As long as trends are moving in their favor, they are comfortable waiting out a problem" because a premature clash could derail China's economic development.[55] That said, if domestic pressures or international ambitions dictate otherwise, China has proven in the past that it will risk war. It will likely be more risk-tolerant in the future, especially if the perceived balance of power tilts in its favor.[56]

---

[51] Devin Thorne and Ben Spevack, *Harbored Ambitions: How China's Port Investments Are Strategically Reshaping the Indo-Pacific*, Washington, D.C.: C4ADS, April 17, 2018.

[52] For example, according to media reports, Chinese personnel at China's military base in Djibouti used lasers to interfere with U.S. military aircraft. Ryan Browne, "Chinese Lasers Injure US Military Pilots in Africa, Pentagon Says," CNN, May 4, 2018.

[53] Interviews with multiple Chinese government-affiliated think tanks, Beijing, June 12–15, 2018.

[54] Xi Jinping, "Secure a Decisive Victory in Building a Moderately Prosperous Society in All Respects and Strive for the Great Success of Socialism with Chinese Characteristics for a New Era," speech delivered at the 19th National Congress of the Communist Party of China, October 18, 2017.

[55] Allison, 2017, p. 146.

[56] See Alastair Iain Johnston, *Cultural Realism: Strategic Culture and Grand Strategy in Chinese History*, Princeton, N.J.: Princeton University Press, 1998.

Implications for the U.S. Air Force and the Future of Warfare

China's rise will pose many challenges to the USAF. First, although different analyses offer different predictions on how and where a U.S.-Chinese conflict might occur, China's emphasis on building a blue-water navy and a multitude of maritime disputes mean that most conflicts in Asia are likely to occur in the maritime domain.[57] As a result, the USAF will need to develop the capabilities to operate at long range (given the expansive geography of Asia, as well as Chinese anti-access/area denial technology) against naval targets (based on the assumption that many of the conflicts will feature contested islands). At the same time, the U.S. military generally and the USAF in particular will also need to think about how to most effectively provide military assistance if the United States were to decide to respond to aggression by sending aid to military partners and allies rather than becoming directly involved in the conflict.

Second, China's economic expansion and large-scale infrastructure investment around the world might create the opportunity for China to establish new military bases and navy access points around the world. China is unlikely to limit itself to one overseas base in Djibouti, and it is important to monitor these attempts to transform economic influence into political leverage.

Third, as the risks of a large-scale, high-end conflict with China increase, so does the value of strategic deterrence. Particularly because it is responsible for two out of three legs of the nuclear triad, the USAF will play a leading role in modernizing and maintaining U.S. deterrence in this new age of great-power competition.

---

[57] See James Dobbins, David C. Gompert, David A. Shlapak, and Andrew Scobell, *Conflict with China: Prospects, Consequences, and Strategies for Deterrence*, Santa Monica, Calif.: RAND Arroyo Center, OP-344-A, 2011; David C. Gompert, Astrid Stuth Cevallos, and Cristina L. Garafola, *War with China: Thinking Through the Unthinkable*, Santa Monica, Calif.: RAND Corporation, RR-1140-A, 2016; Allison, 2017; James Dobbins, Andrew Scobell, Edmund J. Burke, David C. Gompert, Derek Grossman, Eric Heginbotham, and Howard J. Shatz, *Conflict with China Revisited: Prospects, Consequences, and Strategies for Deterrence*, Santa Monica, Calif.: RAND Corporation, PE-248-A, 2017.

Finally, China will remain the main U.S. competitor in the medium and long terms, so the USAF needs to develop expertise on China. Especially as China becomes a more formidable global actor, there will be a continuous need for understanding Chinese capabilities, strategies, and operations.

CHAPTER FOUR

Trend 3: Asia's Reassessment

As China becomes increasingly assertive in the region, Asia faces a stark strategic choice: to balance or bandwagon with Beijing. This, in turn, has profound implications for the U.S. alliance architecture and for the future of conflict in the Indo-Pacific.

Context: Ripe for Rivalry?

Scholars offer split predictions about how Asia will react to China's rise. In his classic essay "Ripe for Rivalry," political scientist Aaron Friedberg argues that "in the long run, it is Asia that seems far more likely [than other regions] to be the cockpit of great-power conflict."[1] Friedberg notes that, compared with Europe, Asia has more authoritarian regimes (China, Russia, North Korea, and Vietnam), more territorial disputes, more historical differences, less economic integration, and fewer international institutions—all making Asia more susceptible to future crises.[2] In a sense, Thucydides' aphorism about the causes of war—that "it was the rise of Athens and the fear that this instilled in Sparta that made the war inevitable"—applies as much to modern Asia reacting to rising China as it did to ancient Greek states.[3]

---

1 Aaron L. Friedberg, "Ripe for Rivalry: Prospects for Peace in a Multipolar Asia," *International Security*, Vol. 18, No. 3, Winter 1993/1994, p. 7.

2 Friedberg, 1993/1994, pp. 15–16, 18, 20, 22.

3 Allison, 2017.

Other scholars are more optimistic. Political scientist David Kang, for example, argues that Asia typically has seen more bandwagoning behavior than balancing behavior, where states preferred accommodating dominant powers to fighting them. Kang observes that "when China has been strong and stable, order has been preserved. East Asian relations have historically been hierarchic, more peaceful, and more stable than those in the West."[4] Others, such as Amitav Acharya, predict a peaceful future for Asia because of growing regional economic interdependence and increasing numbers of multilateral institutions.[5] For a time, this view seemed to better describe the trajectory of geopolitics in Asia, but Friedberg's pessimism increasingly captures recent dynamics in Asia, as we shall see.

Historical Trend: Balancing, Hedging, and Rising Tensions

Across the region, with the notable exceptions of the Philippines and, to a lesser extent, South Korea, much of Asia seems increasingly inclined to push back against Chinese ambitions.

Japan

With an ethnically homogeneous population of 127 million, an estimated gross domestic product (GDP) of $4.8 trillion, and a literacy rate approaching 100 percent, Japan plays a central role in shaping the future of East Asia and faces an increasingly precarious strategic situation.[6] Japan is locked in territorial disputes with Russia over the Kuril Islands, with South Korea over the Liancourt Rocks, and with China over the Senkakus—and none of these disputes shows any sign of being

---

[4] David C. Kang, "Getting Asia Wrong: The Need for New Analytical Frameworks," *International Security*, Vol. 27, No. 4, Spring 2003, p. 66.

[5] Amitav Acharya, "Will Asia's Past Be Its Future?" *International Security*, Vol. 28, No. 3, Winter 2003/2004.

[6] Michael Auslin, *Japanese Internationalism in the 21st Century: Reshaping Foreign Policy in an Era of Upheaval*, Washington, D.C.: American Enterprise Institute, 2017a, pp. 5, 7.

resolved any time soon.[7] So far, Japan seems disinclined to back down. To the contrary, observers often describe Japanese Prime Minister Shinzō Abe as an ardent nationalist. According to Kindai University Professor Carlos Ramirez, "The first two years of this administration, like his first term, focused on returning Japan to a position of leadership in Asia, not only as an economic power, but also as a political and military one."[8]

Despite the "fresh start of relations between Japan and China," the Sino-Japanese rivalry shows no sign of abating.[9] Not only is the territorial dispute between the countries real and the historical animosity deep-seated, but the domestic politics also favor conflict. According to a 2016 Pew study, 86 percent of Japanese and 81 percent of Chinese citizens viewed each other unfavorably.[10] Similarly, Japanese think tank Genron NPO found that in 2016, 71 percent of Japanese and 78 percent of Chinese citizens reported that "relations between their two countries were either bad or relatively bad," and 46.3 percent of Japanese and 71.6 percent of Chinese citizens believed this tension ultimately could lead to conflict.[11]

Japan is already bracing itself for this possibility. Its 2013 *National Security Strategy* noted that Japan "needs to pay careful attention" to China's rise.[12] Japan's 2014 *National Defense Program Guidance*, similarly, called for a "comprehensive defense architecture" for its outly-

---

[7] Auslin, 2017a, p. 45; interviews with Japanese government officials, academics, and think tank analysts, Tokyo, June 18–19, 2018.

[8] Carlos Ramirez, "Abe's Trump Challenge and Japan's Foreign Policy Choices," *The Diplomat*, March 7, 2017.

[9] J. Berkshire Miller, "Japan Warms to China," *Foreign Affairs*, July 17, 2017; Takako Hikotani, "Trump's Gift to Japan," *Foreign Affairs*, Vol. 96, No. 5, September/October 2017; Kiyoshi Takenaka, "Abe Hails 'Fresh Start' to Japan-China Ties After Xi Meeting," Reuters, November 11, 2017.

[10] Auslin, 2017a, p. 108.

[11] Auslin, 2017a, p. 108.

[12] Cabinet Public Relations Office, *National Security Strategy*, Tokyo, December 17, 2013, p. 13.

ing islands.[13] Japanese defense intellectuals likewise argue that Japan "should develop deterrent capabilities of its own," boost defense spending beyond its current 1 percent of GDP, and expand its coast guard to defend its claims in the South and East China seas.[14]

A Sino-Japanese conflict would almost certainly affect the United States. Despite periodic flare-ups over U.S. basing in the country, Japanese foreign elites and the public recognize that "the U.S.-Japanese alliance is the only viable means of guaranteeing Japan's security."[15] In fact, one of the three key objectives in Japan's 2013 *National Security Strategy* is to strengthen the Japanese-U.S. alliance.[16] Consequently, as long as U.S. forces continue to be based in Japan, the security of the two countries will remain intertwined.

India

In theory, India could be the natural counterweight to China. India certainly has a lot of untapped potential—the world's largest population, third largest military, fifth largest defense budget by purchasing power, and seventh largest economy.[17] India also fears growing Chinese influence, sharing a 2,000-mile contested border with China, and has quarreled with China over everything from designating certain Pakistani groups as "global terrorists" in the United Nations Security Council to blocking India's bid to join the Nuclear Suppliers Group.[18] As Hoover

---

13 Auslin, 2017a, p. 27.

14 Japan-US Alliance Study Group, *The Trump Administration and Japan: Challenges and Visions for Japan's Foreign and Security Policy in the New Era*, Tokyo: Institute for International Policy Studies, 2017, pp. 12–14; interviews with Japanese government officials, academics, and think tank analysts, Tokyo, June 18–19, 2018.

15 Hikotani, 2017; interviews with Japanese government officials, academics, and think tank analysts, Tokyo, June 18–19, 2018.

16 Cabinet Public Relations Office, 2013, p. 5.

17 Alyssa Ayres, "Will India Start Acting Like a Global Power? New Delhi's New Role," *Foreign Affairs*, October 16, 2017.

18 K. Alan Kronstad and Shayerah Ilias Akhtar, *India-U.S. Relations: Issues for Congress*, Washington, D.C.: Congressional Research Service, R44876, June 19, 2017, p. 13; Michael Auslin, "Can the Doklam Dispute Be Resolved? The Dangers of China and India's Border Standoff," *Foreign Affairs*, August 1, 2017b.

Institution Asia scholar Michael Auslin notes, "From New Delhi's perspective, China continues to try to encircle it from the north, not only in Bhutan but also through the Sino-Pakistan alliance, which links a growing and aggressive power to India's deadliest enemy."[19]

American-Indian relations have warmed over the years. In 2017, then–Secretary of State Hillary Clinton called India "an indispensable partner and trusted friend," and in 2016, former Pacific Command Commander Admiral Harry Harris had labeled India "the defining partnership for America in the 21st century."[20] To a degree, India has reciprocated these overtures. Indian Prime Minister Narendra Modi skipped the Non-Aligned Summit in Margarita, Venezuela, in September 2016 because Modi recognized it had "outlived its mission and usefulness."[21] India also edged militarily closer to the United States—conducting joint exercises with the United States and, more recently, with Japan.[22] In 2015, India and the United States even issued a "Joint Strategic Vision for the Asia-Pacific and Indian Ocean Region," which included a thinly veiled warning to China and "affirm[ed] the importance of safeguarding maritime security and ensuring freedom of navigation and over flight throughout the region, especially in the South China Sea."[23] And in 2018, in the "2 + 2" dialogue, the United States and India reaffirmed India's status as a Major Defense Partner of the United States, signed a Communications Compatibility and Security Agreement to allow for closer integrations of defense communications, and committed to enhancing defense ties in the future.[24]

---

[19] Auslin, 2017b.

[20] Shane Mason, "India's Achilles' Heel: New Delhi Lags on Defense," *Foreign Affairs*, March 22, 2016; Kronstadt and Akhtar, 2017, p. 1.

[21] Sumit Ganguly, "India After Nonalignment: Why Modi Skipped the Summit," *Foreign Affairs*, September 19, 2016.

[22] Kronstadt and Akhtar, 2017, pp. i, 14, 17.

[23] White House, Office of the Press Secretary, "U.S.-India Joint Strategic Vision for the Asia-Pacific and Indian Ocean Region," Washington, D.C., January 25, 2015.

[24] U.S. Department of State, Office of the Spokesperson, "Joint Statement on the Inaugural U.S.-India 2+2 Ministerial Dialogue," Washington, D.C., September 6, 2018.

And yet, India still lags behind China in multiple ways: 270 million Indians live in extreme poverty and the country needs an estimated $1.5 trillion in infrastructure upgrades—limiting India's ability to invest in military power.[25] Despite its size, much of India's military is relatively poorly equipped.[26] India is also new to power projection, acquiring its first overseas base in the Seychelles only in 2015.[27] Moreover, Washington and New Delhi still differ over Pakistan, Afghanistan, and terrorism—and, although India has shed some of its traditional neutrality, it remains wary of too close a relationship with the United States and formal alliances in general.[28] India also maintains close relations with U.S. adversaries, most notably Russia, and often purchases Russian military equipment—including the S-400 air defense missile system—in defiance of U.S.-led sanctions.[29] In sum, although circumstances might create more opportunities for closer U.S.-Indian military cooperation in the future, India might not be the counterbalance to China that the United States might hope.[30]

Vietnam

Despite being one of only a few notionally communist regimes left in Asia, Vietnam provides a similar case to India, greeting China's rise with apprehension and moving closer to the United States as a result.[31]

---

[25] Ayres, 2017.

[26] Ayres, 2017; Mason, 2016.

[27] Ayres, 2017.

[28] Alyssa Ayres, Elizabeth Economy, and Daniel Markey, "Rebalance the Rebalance: China, India, and the United States," *Foreign Affairs*, July 13, 2016; Ayres, 2017. For an exploration of how the USAF should approach Pakistan, see Jonah Blank, Richard S. Girven, Arzan Tarapore, Julia A. Thompson, and Arthur Chan, *Vector Check Prospects for U.S. and Pakistan Air Power Engagement*, Santa Monica, Calif.: RAND Corporation, RR-2107-AF, 2018.

[29] Rajat Pandit, "India to Go Ahead with S-400 Missile Deal with Russia Despite US Pressure," *Times of India*, July 13, 2018.

[30] For a similar assessment, see Office of the Director of National Intelligence, undated, p. 91.

[31] As Vietnam National University lecturer Le Hong Hiep notes, "Should the CCP fall, the VCP would face enormous challenges in maintaining its power in Vietnam." Le Hong Hiep, "Vietnam's Strategic Trajectory: From Internal Development to External Engagement," *Strategic Insights*, No. 59, June 2012, pp. 2–3, 6.

As Brookings analyst Hunter Marston notes, "For nearly a thousand years, the Chinese forcibly occupied and controlled their less powerful neighbor, throughout which time the Vietnamese fought to expel them."[32] Strategically, control of the disputed Paracel and Spratly islands in the South China Sea is key to Vietnam's ability to defend its 3,260 miles of coastline.[33]

Vietnam also feels Chinese economic pressure. During an annual border exchange in July 2017, the deputy chairman of China's Central Military Commission, General Fan Changlong, threatened to use force against Vietnam if it did not cease oil exploration in the disputed areas of the South China Sea.[34] Hanoi ultimately backed down, but Vietnam cannot afford to abandon its claims in the South China Sea.[35] In 2017, Vietnam National Oil and Gas Group (or PetroVietnam)—the state-run oil company—provided some 10 percent of Vietnam's GDP, much of it from offshore drilling in the South China Sea.[36] As a result, Vietnam is in the midst of a military buildup, both to deter China and to make itself a more attractive regional ally, including with its onetime foe, the United States.[37]

South Korea

South Korea seems to be headed in the opposite direction from Japan, India, and Vietnam. A longtime U.S. ally, South Korea remains ground zero for dealing with its volatile neighbor North Korea, home to some 28,500 U.S. troops and a past troop contributor to the wars in

---

[32] Hunter Marston, "Why Tensions Are Rising Between Vietnam and China," *Foreign Affairs*, August 15, 2017; also see Hong Hiep, 2012, p. 6.

[33] Hong Hiep, 2012, p. 9.

[34] Marston, 2017.

[35] Marston, 2017.

[36] "PetroVietnam Targets 13.28 Million Tonnes of Crude Oil in 2017," *Saigon Online*, July 14, 2017.

[37] Wu Shang-su, "Is Vietnam in Denial on Military Strategy?" *East Asia Forum*, October 30, 2014.

Vietnam, Afghanistan, and Iraq.[38] And yet, South Korea has hedged against China's rise—pursuing warmer ties with China while maintaining a relationship with the United States. China, after all, accounts for 20 percent of South Korea's total trade—more than that of the United States and Japan combined—and has the most economic leverage over North Korea.[39] Indeed, China has wielded this economic stick over South Korea in the past. After South Korea agreed to host a U.S. missile defense system in 2016, Chinese retaliatory sanctions in 2017 cost South Korea $7.5 billion, more than eight and a half times its estimated effect on the Chinese economy.[40]

Political developments could push South Korea further away from the United States, although not necessarily toward China. In May 2017, South Korea elected the left-leaning Minjoo (Democratic) Party's Moon Jae-in as president.[41] Moon argued for a "balanced diplomacy" and rejected the idea of a U.S.–Japanese–South Korean military alliance.[42] Simultaneously, the Trump administration seemingly waffled on U.S. commitment to missile defense in South Korea and renegotiated the five-year-old U.S.-Korea Free Trade Agreement .[43] As a Congressional Research Service report concluded, "[C]hanges resulting from the elections of Donald Trump and Moon Jae-in in 2016 and 2017, respectively, could cause strains that have been relatively dormant for years to reappear."[44] Any ruptures in South Korean alliances could have profound consequences for how the United States handles North

---

[38] Troop figures are as of 2016. Mark E. Manyin, Emma Chanlett-Avery, Mary Beth D. Nikitin, Brock R. Williams, and Jonathan R. Corrado, *U.S.-South Korea Relations*, Washington, D.C.: Congressional Research Service, R41481, May 23, 2017, pp. 11, 18–19, 23.

[39] Manyin et al., 2017, p. 30.

[40] Bonnie S. Glaser and Lisa Collins, "China's Rapprochement with South Korea: Who Won the THAAD Dispute?" *Foreign Affairs*, November 7, 2017.

[41] Manyin et al., 2017, p. 2.

[42] Glaser and Collins, 2017.

[43] Adam Mount, "How to Put the U.S.–South Korean Alliance Back on Track and What to Expect from the Trump-Moon Summit," *Foreign Affairs*, June 28, 2017.

[44] Manyin et al., 2017, p. 1.

Korea, but also for using U.S. bases in South Korea to respond to other threats in Asia.

The Philippines

A former U.S. colony and treaty ally, the Philippines provides an even more extreme example of hedging. In an October 2016 trip to China, Filipino President Rodrigo Duterte proclaimed that "I've realigned myself in your ideological flow," and supposedly offered a three-way alliance with China and Russia.[45] Duterte also threatened to suspend joint military exercises and expel U.S. military personnel from the country.[46]

Behind Duterte's rhetoric are concrete economic considerations. Filipino-Chinese bilateral trade almost doubled between the two countries between 2011 and 2016 (from $12.32 billion to $21.6 billion), and the number of Chinese tourists visiting the Philippines almost tripled over the same period (from 243,137 to 675,663).[47] Above all, Duterte's overtures to China also helped him secure $24 billion in loans from China and the Chinese-backed Asian Infrastructure Investment Bank.[48] Even if Duterte were to be replaced by a leader more supportive of the United States, that leader would still face major economic incentives to maintain a good working relationship with Beijing.

And yet, Duterte's rapprochement with China faces serious headwinds. According to polling in 2015, 91 percent of Filipinos worried about territorial disputes with China.[49] Similarly, according to polling from September 2016, 76 percent of Filipinos trusted the United States,

---

[45] Emily Rauhala, "Duterte Renounces U.S., Declares Philippines Will Embrace China," *Washington Post*, October 20, 2016.

[46] Michael Auslin, "Duterte's Defiance: His Threat to Upend Washington's Pivot to Asia," *Foreign Affairs*, November 2, 2016.

[47] Mayvelin U. Caraballo, "China to Become PH's Principle Trade Partner," *Manila Times*, October 4, 2017.

[48] Jessica C. Liao, "The Filipino Fox: There's a Method to Duterte's Madness," *Foreign Affairs*, January 18, 2017.

[49] Auslin, 2016.

while only 22 percent trusted China.[50] Among business, defense, and political elites, that affinity is even stronger.[51]

Perhaps because of the power of this constituency, the Philippines sued China under the United Nations Convention on the Law of the Seas for its actions in the South China Sea—and in July 2016, the tribunal ruled in favor of the Philippines.[52] Although the court case predated his time in office, Duterte still promised to "personally plant the Filipino flag" on the disputed island of Thitu and ordered the military to fortify its positions on the Spratly Islands.[53] In sum, although the Philippines seems to shun U.S. involvement and to prefer economic cooperation with China today, it might choose to fight Chinese expansion tomorrow.

Future Projection: A 19th-Century Powder Keg?

In predicting the future for Asia, Auslin draws the following analogy: "Current territorial disputes in Asia resemble nineteenth-century European conflicts."[54] Auslin's analogy, if correct, paints a dark portrait of what could lie ahead. There are key differences between the regions (e.g., land-based conflicts versus maritime-centric ones) and the historical periods (e.g., the stabilizing presence of nuclear weapons). Nonetheless, there is enough to the analogy to suggest that Asia faces greater chances of large-scale interstate war in the future.

First, despite Asia's historical aversion to formal alliances, Asian countries are developing nascent military partnerships. Perhaps, the best example is the so-called quad—among the United States, Japan,

---

[50] Liao, 2017.

[51] Richard Javad Heydarian, "Duterte's Dance with China: Why the Philippines Won't Abandon Washington," *Foreign Affairs*, April 26, 2016.

[52] Ronald O'Rourke, *Maritime Territorial and Exclusive Economic Zone (EEZ) Disputes Involving China: Issues for Congress*, Congressional Research Service, R42784, September 15, 2017, p. 21.

[53] Heydarian, 2016.

[54] Auslin, 2017b.

Australia, and India.[55] Japan also sold patrol vessels and airplanes to Malaysia, Vietnam, and the Philippines, and is trying to sell equipment to other countries, including India and Australia.[56] Similarly, Vietnam is expanding its cooperation not only with the United States but with other regional states, such as the Philippines.[57] These relationships stop short of formal alliances, however. Should one country tangle with China, there is no guarantee that others will come to its aid. Ultimately, this could mean that Asia could suffer the worst of both worlds: Without specified security guarantees, these partnerships might not be explicit enough to avoid miscalculation and deter aggression, but, at the same time, they still constitute a sufficient bond to increase the chances that future local wars might spark regional ones.

Second, although many Asian countries concentrated on internal economic development rather than jockeying for regional influence for the past several decades, this might be changing. During the 1980s and 1990s, China focused on internal development rather than on the projection of its power abroad.[58] Similarly, Japan stuck by its pacifist constitution, eschewing military power for political and economic influence.[59] Aside from periodic border clashes with Pakistan, India also mostly concentrated on economic development. In the 1980s, Vietnam adopted the Doi Moi foreign policy, focusing on "developing a multisector market-based economy, renovating the economic structure, stabilizing the socioeconomic environment, promoting science and technology, and opening up the country's foreign relations."[60]

In the future, expansion might once again pay. Always an important trade hub, the East and South China seas are increasingly eco-

---

[55] Interviews with Japanese government officials, academic and think tank analysts, Tokyo, June 18–19, 2018.

[56] Auslin, 2017a, p. 116.

[57] Patrick M. Cronin, Richard Fontaine, Zachary M. Hosford, Oriana Skylar Mastro, Ely Ratner, and Alexander Sullivan, *The Emerging Asia Power Web: The Rise of Bilateral Intra-Asian Security Ties*, Washington, D.C.: Center for a New American Security, 2013, p. 24.

[58] Kang, 2003, p. 68.

[59] Kang, 2003, p. 69.

[60] Hong Hiep, 2012, p. 4.

nomically valuable resources to exploit. Approximately 10 percent of global fish production comes from the South China Sea, and some $3.4 trillion worth of shipping transits these waters.[61] An equally valuable resource might lie beneath the ocean floor. In a region needing energy, the Energy Information Administration estimates there are some 200 million barrels of oil and one to two trillion cubic feet of natural gas reserves in the East China Sea.[62] The South China Sea might hold even greater riches—with an estimated 11 billion barrels of oil and 190 trillion cubic feet of natural gas in reserves.[63]

Finally, like Europe in the 19th and 20th centuries, local debates over sovereignty could spark a regional conflagration. As mentioned, Xi will likely face increasing pressure to reunify with Taiwan in the future, but Taiwan has other ideas. According to Taiwan's National Chengchi University's Election Study Center, Taiwan residents increasingly identify themselves as "Taiwanese" (60.4 percent in 2014 up from 17.6 percent in 1992), and fewer identify as both "Chinese and Taiwanese" (32.7 percent down from 46.4 percent over the same 1992–2014 period).[64] Moreover, those Taiwanese citizens who visited China are more likely to view themselves as a separate nationality.[65] Above all, support for the unification polls in the single digits, and younger Taiwanese are even less enthused about the idea than the older generation.[66] This portends a dark future for cross-strait relations because, as

---

[61] Ronald O'Rourke, *Maritime Territorial and Exclusive Economic Zone (EEZ) Disputes Involving China: Issues for Congress*, Washington, D.C.: Congressional Research Service, R42784, September 15, 2017, pp. 2–3.

[62] O'Rourke, 2017, p. 3.

[63] O'Rourke, 2017, p. 3.

[64] Michael Mazza, "Chinese Check: Forging New Identities in Hong Kong and Taiwan," *The American*, October 14, 2014.

[65] Roselyn Hsueh, "Taiwan's Treaty Trouble: The Backlash Against Taipei's China Deal," *Foreign Affairs*, June 3, 2014.

[66] Mazza, 2014; Salvatore Babones, "Taipei's Name Game: It's Time to Let Taiwan Be Taiwan," *Foreign Affairs*, December 11, 2016.

political scientist Daniel Lynch remarks, "Beijing is unlikely to tolerate Taiwan's de facto independence indefinitely."[67]

A Taiwan conflict, however, would involve more than just Taiwan. Aside from the Taiwan Relations Act, which requires that the United States retain the capacity—though not the obligation—to intervene on behalf of Taiwan, Taiwan's proximity to Japan's southern islands, for example, makes it central to Japanese security as well. As one Japanese academic and adviser to the Japanese government remarked, a Chinese takeover of Taiwan would be "game over for Japan."[68]

Implications for the U.S. Air Force and the Future of Warfare

On a strategic level, the chances that the USAF will end up fighting in Asia will probably increase over coming years, and the region—which has spent more on defense than Europe has since 2012—seems to agree with this generally gloomy prognosis.[69] Several of the aforementioned countries could end up in a conflict with China; given that many of them also enjoy security relationships with the United States, these conflicts could end up involving the United States.

On a political level, the United States' military alliances in Asia will change: Some nations, such as India and Vietnam, will likely develop closer bonds with the United States while others—notably the Philippines and, perhaps, South Korea—could end up in a more precarious relationship. These changes will affect the USAF and the joint force at large in a variety of ways, such as basing and servicing agreements. For example, Vietnam opened its Cam Ranh port to better allow for U.S. naval cooperation, while Duterte's actions jeopardized

---

67 Daniel Lynch, "Why Ma Won the Elections and What's Next for Taiwan and China," *Foreign Affairs*, January 15, 2012.

68 Interview with Japanese academic, Tokyo, June 18, 2018. Other Japanese officials agreed with the sentiment, although in more measured terms. Interviews with Japanese government officials, academics, and think tank analysts, Tokyo, June 18–19, 2018.

69 Cronin et al., 2013, p. 25; Auslin, 2017a, p. 31.

the Enhanced Defense Cooperation Agreement that allowed for greater U.S. access to bases in the Philippines.[70] In the future, then, the United States will need to adjust to these shifting dynamics.

---

[70] Hong Hiep, 2012, p. 11; Auslin, 2016.

CHAPTER FIVE

Trend 4: The Emergence of a Revanchist Russia

While China's rise threatens to upend the dynamic in Asia (and perhaps globally), the United States is also confronting the reemergence of its old nemesis, Russia. After several decades of relative quiet after the Cold War, Russia has become increasingly active, especially in its near abroad.

Context: Russia's Priorities Include Pursuing a Polycentric World

Russia's foreign and defense policies are rooted in the belief that it is a leading international power, albeit a frustrated one. Its most recent set of strategic documents—its Military Doctrine in 2014,[1] *National Security Strategy* in 2015,[2] and *Foreign Policy Concept* in 2016[3]—emphasize Russia's great-power status, its "special responsibility" as one

[1] Ministry of Foreign Affairs of the Russian Federation, Military Doctrine of the Russian Federation, No. Pr.-2976, December 25, 2014.

[2] *Strategiya natsional'noi bezopasnosti Rossiiskoi Federatsii [National Security Strategy of the Russian Federation]*, Decree of the President of the Russian Federation, No. 683, December 31, 2015.

[3] Ministry of Foreign Affairs of the Russian Federation, *Kontseptsiya vneshnei politiki Rossiiskoi Federatsii [Foreign Policy Concept of the Russian Federation]*, approved by President of the Russian Federation Vladimir Putin on November 30, 2016, December 1, 2016.

of the major nuclear powers, and its determination to "increase its role in the polycentric world."[4] These core beliefs have several implications.

First, Russia remains acutely sensitive to U.S. and NATO threats.[5] Russia consistently lists capabilities that threaten its nuclear capability—such as the U.S. missile defense system in Europe and the Prompt Global Strike Concept—as key threats to not only Russia's security, but also its great-power status, which is bound up in its nuclear capability.[6] Unsurprisingly, in March 2018, Russian President Vladimir Putin unveiled several new nuclear strike systems that "can penetrate any existing and future missile defense systems."[7]

Second, Russia views democratic revolutions as Western-sponsored attempts to undermine legitimate regimes. Russia views the color revolutions in Georgia (2003), Ukraine (2004), and Kyrgyzstan (2005); the Arab Spring; and the Ukrainian Revolution of Dignity (2014) as foreign-inspired attempts to install pro-West regimes. Russia similarly viewed the 2011–2013 protests in its own country as supported by the United States and the West.[8] Importantly, the Kremlin often links revolutions in its neighborhood to the threat of color revolutions at home.[9]

Third, Russia wants to expand its economic and political influence, particularly in its near abroad, through the Eurasian Economic Union, Collective Security Treaty Organization, and the Com-

---

4 *Strategiya natsional'noi bezopasnosti Rossiiskoi Federatsii [National Security Strategy of the Russian Federation]*, 2015, Chapter Two, paragraph 7.

5 *Strategiya natsional'noi bezopasnosti Rossiiskoi Federatsii [National Security Strategy of the Russian Federation]*, 2015.

6 Vladimir Putin, "Poslanie Prezidenta Federal'nomu Sobraniyu" ["President's Message to the Federal Assembly"], Kremlin.ru, December 4, 2014.

7 Vladimir Putin, "Poslanie Prezidenta Federal'nomu Sobraniyu" ["President's Message to the Federal Assembly"], Kremlin.ru, March 1, 2018.

8 Ivan Egorov, "Patrushev: Popytki ustroit' "tsvetnye revolyutsii" v Rossii besperspektivny" ["Patrushev: Attempts to Incite 'Color Revolutions' in Russia Are Useless"], *Rossiskaya Gazeta*, May 18, 2017.

9 Valerii Gerasimov, Tsennost' nauki v predvidenii" ["The Value of Science Is in Foresight'], *Voenno-Promyshlennyi Kurer [Military Industrial Courier]*, February 27, 2013.

monwealth of Independent States.[10] From an economic perspective, Russia appears to believe that Eurasian integration is its only chance to become an "independent center of global development."[11] From a security perspective, regional integration allows Russia to keep hostile powers farther away from its borders, maintain the Commonwealth of Independent States' Joint Air Defense, combat such threats as terrorism and transnational crime, and prevent "color revolutions" in its near abroad.[12]

Finally, Russia sees itself as the protector of Russians abroad. Russia offered citizenship to the Russophile inhabitants of Crimea, Donetsk, Luhansk, Abkhazia, South Ossetia, and Transnistria and committed to protecting "compatriots"—not only Russian citizens, but also ethnic Russians or just Russian speakers—sometimes with military force, if necessary.[13]

Historical Trend: Russia's Use of Force

These priorities have shaped where and how Russia uses force in the post–Cold War period. In Russia's first large-scale use of military force after the collapse of the Soviet Union, Russia tried to crush an independence movement in Chechnya in December 1994, sparking the First Chechen War.[14] The Russia intervention turned into a debacle, and, in 1997, Russia gave the separatists de facto control over

---

[10] Ministry of Foreign Affairs of the Russian Federation, 2016.

[11] Vladimir Putin, "Vystuplenie na zasedanii kluba "Valdai"" ["Speech at the Valdai Club Meeting"], September 19, 2013.

[12] Vladimir Zakharov, "Sostoyanie i perspektivy razvitiya Organizatsii Dogovora o kollektivnoi bezopasnosti" ["The State and Development Prospects of the Collective Security Treaty Organization"], *PROBLEMY NATSIONAL'NOI STRATEGII [Problems and National Strategies]*, Vol. 3, No. 12, 2012.

[13] Agnia Grigas, *Beyond Crimea: The New Russian Empire*, New Haven, Conn.: Yale University Press, 2016. Chapter 3 provides a comprehensive overview of the origins and the development of Russia's compatriot policies.

[14] For an in-depth discussion of the Chechen Wars, see John Russell, *Chechnya-Russia's 'War on Terror,'* London: Routledge, 2007; Anna Politkovskaya, *A Small Corner of Hell: Dispatches*

the region. In 1999, then–Prime Minister Vladimir Putin accused Chechen secessionists of terrorist attacks in Moscow, prompting the Second Chechen War.[15] Putin also believed that the United States provided significant political, financial, and operational aid to Chechen terrorists to weaken Russia.[16] After a brutal early campaign followed by a protracted counterinsurgency, Putin declared the conflict terminated in 2009.[17] The Chechen wars defined Putin's first two terms as president, helping him consolidate his power at home. The conflicts also underscore that Russia will use force if it perceives a threat to the regime's stability.

Russia's first major contested deployment of armed force outside the borders of the Russian Federation occurred during the 1999 Kosovo War.[18] Russia had long-standing cultural ties with Serbia and saw NATO's intervention as an attempt to expand its geopolitical sphere of influence farther east, not as a humanitarian operation.[19] Nonetheless, Russia initially limited its involvement to mediating the conflict to guarantee Yugoslavia's sovereignty,[20] until events drove Russia to reconsider. After a brief but intense air campaign by NATO, Serbian leader

---

from Chechnya, Chicago: University of Chicago Press, 2007; and Mark Galeotti, *Russia's Wars in Chechnya 1994–2009*, Oxford, UK: Osprey, 2014.

[15] Chechen involvement in the attacks was never proven, while there is abundant evidence that Russian authorities were complicit in the attacks. For details, see John Dunlop, *The Moscow Bombings of September 1999: Examinations of Russian Terrorist Attacks at the Onset of Vladimir Putin's Rule*, Vol. 110, New York: Columbia University Press, 2014.

[16] "Putin rasskazal, kak SShA podderzhivali terroristov v Chechne" ["Putin Told How U.S. Were Supporting Chechen Terrorists"], *Ria Novosti*, June 13, 2017.

[17] Michael Schwirtz, "Russia Ends Operations in Chechnya," *New York Times*, April 16, 2009.

[18] Russia also conducted various smaller interventions in the civil conflicts in Georgia, Transnistria, and Tajikistan in the early 1990s without a direct possibility of a clash with the West.

[19] Andrei P. Tsygankov, *Russia's Foreign Policy: Change and Continuity in National Identity*, Lanham, Md.: Rowman & Littlefield, 2016, p. 112.

[20] Robert Brannon, *Russian Civil-Military Relations*, Farnham, UK: Ashgate, 2009, pp. 73–99.

Slobodan Milosevic accepted an international peace plan.[21] Russia did not receive an independent sector for peacekeeping and sent a column of several dozen armored vehicles to occupy the Slatina airport to block the arrival of the NATO peacekeeping force. Ultimately, NATO and Russia reached a diplomatic solution, but the Kosovo intervention highlights Russia's willingness to gamble on a possible military confrontation with NATO if it perceives its national interests are at stake.[22]

In August 2008, Russia fought a brief but intense war with Georgia.[23] Russia viewed Georgia's pro-American, pro-NATO, and European Union (EU)–oriented government as a Western proxy.[24] Before the conflict, Russian leadership repeatedly declared that Russia "will do everything" to prevent the accession of Georgia into NATO.[25] Russia was also concerned with the fate of pro-Russia minorities in the breakaway regions of South Ossetia and Abkhazia.[26] After Georgia and South Ossetian separatists exchanged artillery fire, Russian forces occupied South Ossetia and several Georgian cities. To

[21] NATO, Statement by NATO Secretary General Dr. Javier Solana on Suspension of Air Operations, press release 093, June 10, 1999.

[22] A. Krechetnikov, "Brosok na Prishtinu: na grani voiny" ["March to Pristina: At the Brink of War"], Russkaya Sluzhba BBC, June 11, 2014.

[23] For a detailed overview of the conflict, see Svante E. Cornell and S. Frederick Starr, eds., *The Guns of August 2008*, Armonk, N.Y.: ME Sharpe, 2009; Ronald Asmus, *A Little War That Shook the World: Georgia, Russia, and the Future of the West*, New York: St. Martin's Press, 2010; and Ariel Cohen and Robert E. Hamilton, *The Russian Military and the Georgia War: Lessons and Implications*, Carlisle, Pa.: Strategic Studies Institute, 2011.

[24] When asked during a 2004 press conference about visits of high-ranking Russian officials to Abkhazia, Vladimir Putin replied: "[Y]ou linked Georgian leadership with the West. Is it because they [Georgian leadership] are receiving their salaries from Soros?" "Press-konferentsiya Vladimira Putina dlya rossiiskikh i inostrannykh zhurnalistov" ["Vladimir Putin's Press Conference for Russian and Foreign Journalists"], Kremlin.ru, December 23, 2004.

[25] Foreign minister Lavrov quoted in "RF sdelaet vse, chtoby ne dopustit' prinjatija Ukrainy i Gruzii v NATO" ["Russian Federation Will Do Everything to Prevent Accession of Ukraine and Georgia to NATO"], *Ria Novosti*, April 8, 2008.

[26] Jim Nichol, *Russia-Georgia Conflict in South Ossetia: Context and Implications for U.S. Interests*, Washington, D.C.: Congressional Research Service, RL34618, August 29, 2008.

further cement its regional foothold, Russia signed a joint force agreement with Abkhazia in 2016 and with Armenia in 2017.[27]

Ultimately, the Georgia war foreshadowed the Ukraine conflict, in which Russia, again, intervened to prevent perceived Western encroachment and protect Russian populations. When protesters ousted President Viktor Yanukovych after he rejected an EU association agreement in 2014, Russia viewed it as a U.S.-sponsored coup meant to deprive Russia of its "legitimate" sphere of influence.[28] In response, Russian troops seized Crimea, citing concern for Russian citizens and Russian speakers in the region, and formally annexed it after a hastily conducted referendum. Russia also deployed significant military forces in Ilovaisk in 2014 and Debaltseve in 2014 in Eastern Ukraine. Unlike in the Crimea, however, the war in the Donbass bogged down in a stalemate. As of 2017, Russia planned to station a considerable number of troops along the border with Ukraine and had not ruled out the possibility of escalating the conflict.[29]

In 2015, Russia intervened in the Syrian civil war—its most significant intervention in the Middle East in decades. Russia claimed it wanted to fight terrorism, but other motives were also apparent.[30] According to Russia's defense minister, the military intervention solved

---

[27] Colonel General Vladimir Shamanov, head of the State Duma Defense Committee, quoted in Dmitri Sergeev, "Koshmarnyi son Tbilisi: kak otreagiruet Rossiya v sluchae agressii protiv Abkhazii" ["Tbilisi's Nightmare: How Russia Will React in Case of Aggression Against Abkhazia"], tvzvezda.ru, March 11, 2016; "Putin ratifitsiroval soglashenie RF i Abkhazii ob ob"edinennoi gruppirovke voisk" ["Putin Ratified the Agreement Between RF and Abkhazia on 'Joint Force'"], Interfax.ru, November 22, 2016; "Armeniya ratifitsirovala soglashenie s RF ob ob"edinennoi gruppirovke voisk" ["Armenia Ratified the Agreement with RF on Joint Force"], Interfax.ru, October 5, 2017.

[28] Elena Chernenko, "«Za destabilizatsiei Ukrainy skryvaetsya popytka radikal'nogo oslableniya Rossii». Sekretar' Sovbeza RF Nikolai Patrushev o glavnykh ugrozakh dlya bezopasnosti Rossii" ["'The Destabilization of Ukraine Hides an Attempt to Radically Weaken Russia": Secretary of the Russian Security Council Nikolai Patrushev on the Main Threats to Russia's Security"], Kommersant.ru, June 22, 2015.

[29] International Institute for Strategic Studies, *The Military Balance 2017*, London: February 2017, pp. 184–185.

[30] R. Batyrshin, "Interv'yu Vladimira Putina teleradiokompanii «Mir»" ["Interview of Vladimir Putin on the Mir TV and Radio Company"], Kremlin.ru, April 12, 2017.

"the geopolitical task of interrupting the chain of 'color revolutions' in the Middle East and Africa."[31] Russia also wanted to protect and expand its military bases in in Tartus and Hmeimim.[32] Economically, the intervention showcased Russian military hardware and boosted its arms sales to the region and potentially increased Russia's influence in the Middle East and sway over global energy prices.[33] Finally, Moscow felt that intervening could divert international attention away from Ukraine, giving Russia additional leverage against the United States and its allies.[34]

Russia's intervention in Syria featured one of the few direct military engagements between U.S. and Russian personnel. On February 7, 2017, a group of forces allied with Assad combined with a large number of Russian mercenaries working for the Wagner private military company with suspected links to the Russian state—although the Kremlin denied knowledge of this operation—attacked U.S.and

---

[31] Ministry of Defense of the Russian Federation, "Ministr oborony Rossii vystupil s lektsiei na otkrytii II Vserossiiskogo molodezhnogo foruma v MGIMO," ["Russian Defense Minister Gave a Lecture at the Opening of the II All-Russian Youth Forum at MGIMO"], February 21, 2017a.

[32] Shoigue quoted by Ministry of Defense of the Russian Federation, Twitter, 3 a.m., December 26, 2017b.

[33] The head of Russia's largest defense conglomerate and a close associate of Putin, Sergei Chemezov, said, "As for the conflict situation in the Middle East, I do not hide it and everyone understands that the more conflicts there are in the region, the more they buy our weapons. Volumes of arms exports in our country continue to grow, regardless of sanctions. Basically, it is Latin America and the Middle East." "Glava 'Rostekha' soobshchil o roste prodazh: 'Chem bol'she konfliktov, tem bol'she u nas pokupayut vooruzheniya'" ["The Head of Rostech on Growing Arms Sales: 'The More Conflicts There Are, the More They Buy Our Weapons'"], News.ru, February 23, 2015; Dmitrii Trenin, "Rossija na Blizhnem Vostoke: zadachi, prioritety, politicheskie stimuly" ["Russia in the Middle East: Tasks, Priorities, Political Incentives"], Moscow: Carnegie Moscow Center, April 21, 2016; Mehul Srivastava and Erika Solomon, "Israel Launches Air Strikes Deep Within Syria," *Financial Times*, February 10, 2018.

[34] Institute for Strategic Studies, 2017, p. 183; "Shojgu: rasshirenie prisutstvija RF v Mirovom okeane trebuetsja iz-za nestabil'noj obstanovki" ["Shoigu: Russia Should Expand Its Military Presence in the World Ocean Due to the Unstable (Security) Situation"], Tass.ru, October 27, 2017.

Kurdish forces near an oil field in Syria, resulting in a firefight that left hundreds dead.[35]

Russia also has employed a wide range of tools that fall below the conventional threshold of conflict, ranging from influence operations to cyberattacks.[36] Some of these operations have been quite brazen, such as interference in the 2016 U.S. presidential election or the attempted assassination of a former Russian spy in March 2018 in the UK.[37]

As this brief history suggests, Russia will use force when the regime is threatened, when the West encroaches on its sphere of influence, or when its compatriots are ostensibly threatened. Moreover, Russia has repeatedly shown a willingness to gamble on conflict with the West. The Russia political system, however, arguably favors risk-taking and allows for secretive and swift action.[38]

Future Projection: The Return of a More Assertive Russia

Russia will almost certainly continue on its current strategic course, especially after Putin's reelection in March 2018 for another six-year term. Economic circumstances, however, will constrain Russia's actions. The Russian economy is growing despite lower oil prices and Western sanctions, but the International Monetary Fund reported in 2018 that "Russia's convergence to advanced economy income levels

---

[35] For a detailed discussion of the attack and links to original sources see Neil Hauer, "Russia's Mercenary Debacle in Syria: Is the Kremlin Losing Control?" *Foreign Affairs*, February 26, 2018.

[36] Linda Robinson, Todd C. Helmus, Raphael S. Cohen, Alireza Nader, Andrew Radin, Madeline Magnuson, and Katya Migacheva, *Modern Political Warfare: Current Practices and Possible Responses*, Santa Monica, Calif.: RAND Corporation, RR-1772-A, 2017; Office of the Director of National Intelligence, "Assessing Russian Activities and Intentions in Recent US Elections," Washington, D.C., Intelligence Community Assessment, January 6, 2017.

[37] "Russian Spy: Highly Likely Moscow Behind Attack, Says Theresa May," BBC News, March 13, 2018.

[38] Dmitrii Trenin, *Avoiding U.S.-Russia Military Escalation During the Hybrid War*, Moscow: Carnegie Endowment for International Peace, January 2018.

has stalled and its weight in the global economy is shrinking."[39] The net result, therefore, might be the return of a more assertive Russia, but not an all-powerful one.

Russia's efforts will probably revolve around the post-Soviet space. Given Russia's fears of "color revolutions," it could intervene in the affairs of any of the Collective Security Treaty Organization members—Armenia, Belarus, Kazakhstan, Kyrgyzstan, and Tajikistan—if popular unrest ever threatens pro-Russian regimes in these countries. For similar reasons, Russia will likely maintain strong economic, political, and military support for the breakaway regions of Donetsk and Luhansk in Ukraine, Abkhazia and South Ossetia in Georgia, and (to a lesser extent) Transnistria in Moldova.

Russia's development of long-range strike, air defense, and rapidly deployable forces—as well as its integration with local proxies and private military companies—will also open the possibility of limited expeditionary operations.[40] Although there are no immediate indications that Russia will conduct another expeditionary operation, it might do so if it sees a suitable opening. After all, Russian leadership and military theorists emphasize offensive capabilities, swift action, and deception as essential elements of the future wars.[41]

Above all, Russia will probably emphasize "active measures," such as cyber operations and influence campaigns, to influence domestic developments in the United States and other Western democracies as a way to change their foreign policy priorities and cause rifts in the NATO alliance. Despite the economic and military power asymmetry between Russia and the United States, Russia believes that it can

---

[39] International Monetary Fund, European Department, *Russian Federation: 2018 Article IV Consultation—Press Release; Staff Report*, Paris, September 12, 2018.

[40] Andrew Radin, Lynn E. Davis, Edward Geist, Eugeniu Han, Dara Massicot, Matthew Povlock, Clint Reach, Scott Boston, Samuel Charap, William Mackenzie, Katya Migacheva, Trevor Johnston, and Austin Long, *The Future of the Russian Military: Russia's Ground Combat Capabilities and Implications for U.S.-Russia Competition*, Santa Monica, Calif.: RAND Corporation, RR-3099-A, 2019.

[41] I. Popov and M. Khamzatov, *Voina budushchego. Kontseptual'nye osnovy i prakticheskie vyvody [The War of the Future: Conceptual Foundations and Practical Considerations]*, Moscow: Kuchkovo Pole, 2016.

eventually win the competition with the United States through these measures, without the costs of direct military intervention.[42]

Implications for the U.S. Air Force and the Future of Warfare

Russia's resurgence has important implications for the USAF and the joint force. First, given the size and capabilities of Russian military forces on NATO's eastern borders, the USAF will need to reassess its posture in Europe for both reassurance and deterrence. Russia might respond to these actions by using hybrid measures ranging from inciting local protests around military bases to more-direct measures, such as cyber-attacks.[43] Consequently, although the USAF needs to prepare for high-end conventional combat against Russia, the USAF and the joint force will need to further explore their roles in countering these unconventional tactics specifically and gray-zone operations in general.

Second, perhaps to an even greater extent than China, the emergence of revanchist Russia—with its emphasis on nuclear weapons—will require, in turn, that the United States as a whole and the USAF in particular place a renewed emphasis on modernizing and maintaining a nuclear arsenal.

Third, as demonstrated by the events in Ukraine and Georgia, the United States has responded to Russian aggression by sending aid to its regional allies and partners rather than by getting directly involved militarily with a nuclear armed adversary. Consequently, it is incumbent on the U.S. military to ensure such assistance to its allies.

Fourth, managing a resurgent Russia will require personnel with a good understanding of that country. During the Cold War, the USAF developed and maintained a cadre of officers with compre-

---

[42] In a recent interview, Putin expressed confidence that Russia will prevail in the competition with the West in the long run. V. Solov'ev, "Miroporyadok 2018" ["World Order 2018"], True TV, March 22, 2018.

[43] Christopher Paul and Miriam Matthews, *The Russian "Firehose of Falsehood" Propaganda Model: Why It Might Work and Options to Counter It*, Santa Monica, Calif.: RAND Corporation, PE-198-OSD, 2016.

hensive regional expertise and understanding of the Soviet Union as a military opponent. Given the risks of conflict with Russia, the USAF will need officers with similar expertise regarding Russia and its near abroad to inform decisionmakers and avoid miscalculation.[44]

Finally, Russia's reemergence will pose a host of operational challenges. Russian weaponry, particularly air defense systems, will pose challenges for the USAF in the event of conflict in Europe and, potentially, in the Middle East.[45] Even when Russian forces are not directly involved, Russia's willingness to sell these systems to other actors, including Iran, could affect the USAF's ability to project power against other adversaries.[46]

---

[44] Risky maneuvers of Russian military aircraft around U.S./NATO aircraft have been documented on numerous occasions. Julian E. Barnes, "U.S. Seeks Better Deterrence in Europe Against Russian Aircraft," *Wall Street Journal*, April 21, 2016.

[45] "S-400, Pantsir Air Defense Systems Protect Russian Air Group in Syria 24/7," *Sputnik*, April 7, 2017.

[46] F. Gady, "Iran Deploys New Russian Air Defense System Around Nuclear Site," *The Diplomat*, August 31, 2016.

CHAPTER SIX

Trend 5: Upheaval in Europe

As Russia reemerges as a threat to Europe—and, potentially, to international security—Europe risks becoming increasingly fragmented and absorbed with its own challenges. Security in Europe depends on unity within NATO—the primary alliance framework between the United States and Europe, which operates based on consensus—and within the EU. After all, the EU handles crises within its borders, not NATO. For instance, the European Border and Coast Guard Agency (Frontex) is the main agency dealing with the migrant crisis; the European Union Agency for Law Enforcement Cooperation's European Counter Terrorism Center leads domestic counterterrorism operations and facilitates intelligence-gathering and intelligence-sharing across European borders.[1] The EU also enables a coordinated response to many Russian gray-zone tactics, such as disinformation campaigns and interference in electoral processes. Although recent EU initiatives, such as the European Defence Fund and Permanent Structured Cooperation in Defence, have yet to yield positive results, they still might be Europe's best chance to maximize its limited defense spending.[2] By contrast, a fragmented EU might draw European attention inward and sap

---

[1] European Union Agency for Law Enforcement Cooperation, "European Counter Terrorism Centre—ECTC," webpage, undated; Council of the European Union, "EU Fight Against Terrorism," webpage, March 20, 2018.

[2] Interviews with German government officials, Berlin, April 20, 2018; interview with Polish think tank, Warsaw, April 23, 2018.

defense resources.[3] Europe confronts a series of political challenges—migration, terrorism, political turmoil, and a resurgent Russia—on top of the economic challenges of the Euro crisis, all of which threaten to undermine the EU's ability to respond effectively to these threats and which could alter the U.S. alliance.[4]

Context: An Uncertain Future for Europe

Scholars predict several possible scenarios for the future of the EU, such as "muddling through";[5] a "two-speed" or "multispeed" EU;[6] an EU divided into balanced, opposing blocs;[7] a more-integrated EU;[8] a less integrated but possibly enlarged EU;[9] and a disintegrated EU.[10] Most, however, envision a future that falls somewhere between the two most extreme scenarios, in which the EU remains divided but still muddles through. There is no question, however, that the EU faces severe challenges today.

---

[3] Maria Carmen Martin Palacios, "What Would Happen to Security in Europe If the European Union Broke Up?" *Sigma Iota Rho Journal of International Relations*, September 27, 2017.

[4] Rem Korteweg, "The EU and Transatlantic Relations," Centre for European Reform, February 20, 2013.

[5] Kristin Archick, *The European Union: Current Challenges and Future Prospects*, Washington, D.C.: Congressional Research Service, R44249, February 27, 2017, p. 17; Thomas Raines, Matthew Goodwin, and David Cutts, *The Future of Europe: Comparing Public and Elite Attitudes*, London: Chatham House, June 2017, p. 35.

[6] Archick, 2017, p. 18; John Peet, "Creaking at 60: The Future of the European Union," *The Economist*, March 25, 2017.

[7] Ministry of Defence, *Strategic Trends Programme: Global Strategic Trends—Out to 2045*, London, April 30, 2014, p. 119.

[8] Archick, 2017, p. 18; Jan Techau, "Four Predictions on the Future of Europe," *Judy Dempsey's Strategic Europe*, Carnegie Europe blog, January 12, 2016.

[9] Ministry of Defence, 2014, p. 118; Archick, 2017, p. 18.

[10] Ian Morris, "Why Europe's Great Experiment Is Failing," Stratfor, January 27, 2016; John Gillingham and Marian L. Tupy, "The EU Will Likely Implode," *The National Interest*, February 25, 2016; Gwythian Prins, "The EU Is at Clear Risk of Collapse—And the 'Remainiacs' Just Don't See It," *Briefings for Brexit*, April 2018.

Historical Trend: Migration, Terrorism, Political Turmoil, and Russia

Over the past decade, public dissatisfaction with the EU has increased among Europeans.[11] A recent report by Chatham House found that while 71 percent of European elites felt the EU benefited them, there is "simmering discontent within the public, large sections of whom view the EU in negative terms, want to see it return some powers to member states, and feel anxious over the effects of immigration."[12] Only 34 percent of the public across EU member states felt they benefited from EU membership, and 54 percent felt their countries were better places to live 20 years ago.[13] This decline of faith is largely attributable to one major economic issue—the continued economic fallout from the Eurozone Crisis and the subsequent austerity measures that were incorporated in an attempt to control rising public debt that hit such countries as Greece, Portugal, Italy, and Spain particularly hard—and four geopolitical factors: migration, terrorism, political turmoil, and a revanchist Russia.[14]

Migrant Crisis

Beginning with a sudden spike in immigration in 2015—primarily in the number of economic migrants from Africa and the Middle East—the migration crisis presents the most severe political and security threat to the future of Europe.[15] In 2015 and 2016, 2.5 million people applied for asylum in EU countries, with an additional 2.2 million people found

[11] Interviews with British government officials, London, April 16, 2018; interviews with NATO officials, London, April 18, 2018.

[12] Raines, Goodwin, and Cutts, 2017, p. 2.

[13] Raines, Goodwin, and Cutts, 2017, p. 2.

[14] For a summary, see Kristin Archick, *The European Union: Questions and Answers*, Washington, D.C.: Congressional Research Service, RS21372, September 7, 2018, pp. 4–5.

[15] Office of the United Nations High Commissioner for Refugees, *Mixed Migration Trends in Libya: Changing Dynamics and Protection Challenges*, Geneva: July 2017, p. 59; Rebecca Flood, "Shock Figures: Seven Out of 10 Migrants Crossing to Europe Are Not Refugees, UN Reveals," *Daily Express*, July 4, 2017; interview with London think tank, April 17, 2018; interviews with EU officials, Brussels, April 19, 2018; interviews with German government officials, Berlin, April 20, 2018; interview with Polish think tank, Warsaw, April 23, 2018.

to be illegally present in 2015.[16] The latest EU data indicate that "the number of people residing in an EU Member State with citizenship of a non-member country on 1 January 2017 was 21.6 million, representing 4.2 percent of the EU-28 population."[17]

Although the flow of migrants has subsided somewhat, the divisions caused by the influx linger on. This migrant crisis pitted EU officials and pro-migration powers, such as Germany, against the Visegrád Group (V4), consisting of Hungary, Slovakia, Poland, and the Czech Republic; Italy; and Austria.[18] Although Germany stated it would accept an unlimited number of migrants, the V4 countries refused to comply with the EU's mandatory quotas.[19] In response, the European Parliament proposed fining countries €250,000 for each migrant they refused to accept.[20] Although the EU never imposed these fines, the EU Commission is suing Hungary, Poland, and the Czech Republic in the European Court of Justice for failing to comply with migrant quotas and relocation plans.[21]

Attempts to discuss solutions to the crisis have only deepened these rifts. For instance, the EU Commission convened an "emergency summit on migration" on June 24, 2018, but declined to invite the V4 countries.[22] Countries that did attend the summit were frustrated by the outcome, with Italy's interior minister Matteo Salvini even

---

[16] European Parliament, "EU Migrant Crisis: Facts and Figures," news blog, June 30, 2017.

[17] Eurostat, "Migration and Migrant Population Statistics," webpage, undated.

[18] Steven Erlanger, "Migration to Europe Is Slowing, but the Political Issue Is as Toxic as Ever," *New York Times*, June 22, 2018; "Where Do EU Countries Stand on Migration?" *Deutsche Welle*, June 22, 2018.

[19] Alistair Walsh, "Chancellor Angela Merkel Rejects Refugee Limit for Germany in TV Interview," *Deutsche Welle*, July 16, 2017.

[20] Stefano M. Torelli, "Ideology First: Italy's Troubled Approach to Migration," European Council on Foreign Relations, June 11, 2018.

[21] "EU to Sue Poland, Hungary, and Czechs for Refusing Refugee Quotas," BBC, December 7, 2017.

[22] Lili Bayer and Jacopo Barigazzi, "Central Europeans to Boycott Migration Summit They Weren't Invited to," *Politico*, June 21, 2018.

"threaten[ing] to stop Rome's contributions to the EU budget if he [is] unable to secure a favourable shift in migration policy."[23]

The lack of an effective response to the migrant crisis has fueled political turmoil within many EU states. Notably, the latest elections in Italy brought into power two anti-immigration, euroskeptic parties, the League and the 5 Star Movement.[24] Clashing stances on migration have even threatened to disband German Chancellor Angela Merkel's ruling coalition.[25]

Terrorism

Terrorism—which is often, if inaccurately, linked to the migrant crisis—has also exacerbated political tensions across Europe. Although the terrorist threat comes primarily from homegrown jihadists, a median 59 percent of European publics express the belief that the migrant crisis will increase the terrorism threat in their countries.[26] In fairness, asylum-seekers allegedly perpetrated at least four terrorist attacks between January 2016 and April 2017.[27] Moreover, at least 1,500 ISIS-linked foreign fighters have returned to their European countries of origin, sometimes without government knowledge, and can operate largely unencumbered across national borders within the Schengen Area.[28] For example, foreign fighter returnees used Molen-

---

23 Alex Barker and James Politi, "Brussels Draws Fire from Rome over Migration Proposals," *Financial Times*, June 20, 2018.

24 James Politi, "Five Star and League Take Power in Italy," *Financial Times*, June 1, 2018.

25 Guy Chazan, "CDU-CSU Spat Shakes Europe's Most Successful Electoral Alliance," *Financial Times*, June 18, 2018.

26 Aaron Williams, "How Two Brussels Neighborhoods Became 'a Breeding Ground' for Terror," *Washington Post*, April 1, 2016; Richard Wike, Bruce Stokes, and Katie Simmons, "Europeans Fear Wave of Refugees Will Mean More Terrorism, Fewer Jobs," Pew Global Research Center, July 11, 2016.

27 Manni Crone, Maja Felicia Falkentoft, and Teemu Tammikko, *European Citizens, Not Refugees, Behind Most Terrorist Attacks in Europe*, Copenhagen: Danish Institute for International Studies, June 21, 2017.

28 Peter Bergen, David Sterman, Alyssa Sims, and Albert Ford, *ISIS in the West: The Western Militant Flow to Syria and Iraq*, Washington, D.C.: New America, policy paper, March 2016; Crone, Falkentoft, and Tammikko, 2017; Thomas Renard and Rik Coolsaet, eds.,

beek, Belgium, as a hub to plan the November 2015 and March 2016 attacks in Paris and Brussels, respectively.[29]

Terrorism has also undermined publics' faith in their governments and further divided European states.[30] Several polls show that up to 82 percent of EU publics feel their governments are not handling terrorism adequately.[31] After the Paris attacks, French officials reprimanded the Belgian government for failing to address radicalization activity within its borders.[32] France also turned to the EU rather than NATO for assistance because "an appeal to NATO would have required a level of cooperation that French officials felt Washington was unlikely to offer quickly, and with Paris bleeding, the French weren't prepared to wait."[33] Indeed, some NATO officials believe that responding to domestic terrorism does not even fall under NATO's mandate.[34]

Political Turmoil

Although German and EU officials view nationalism as dangerous and favor a pan-European identity, nationalism is on the rise across

Returnees: Who Are They, Why Are They (Not) Coming Back and How Should We Deal with Them? Brussels: Egmont Institute, February 2018, p. 71. The Schengen Area encompasses 26 European states (Austria, Belgium, Czech Republic, Denmark, Estonia, Finland, France, Germany, Greece, Hungary, Iceland, Italy, Latvia, Liechtenstein, Lithuania, Luxembourg, Malta, Netherlands, Norway, Poland, Portugal, Slovakia, Slovenia, Spain, Sweden, and Switzerland) that have officially abolished all types of border control.

[29] "Unraveling the Connections Among the Paris Attackers," *New York Times*, March 18, 2016.

[30] Interview with British think tank, London, April 17, 2018; interviews with EU officials, Brussels, April 19, 2018; interviews with German government officials, Berlin, April 20, 2018; interview with Polish think tank, Warsaw, April 23, 2018.

[31] European Parliament, "Survey: People Reveal Their Priorities for the EU," news blog, January 7, 2016; "France's Response to Terrorism: Loss of Faith," *The Economist*, July 30, 2016.

[32] Peter Spiegel, "Paris Attacks: Belgium Cries Foul over French Blame Game," *Financial Times*, November 18, 2015.

[33] Ian Bremmer, "The Hollow Alliance," *Time*, June 16, 2016.

[34] Interviews with NATO officials, Brussels, April 18, 2018.

Europe.[35] The Polish, Hungarian, Austrian, and Italian governments, for instance, stress national sovereignty and rail against EU encroachment on their domestic affairs.[36] Eastern European countries also claim they are stigmatized by the EU as "backward-looking, autocratic, neo-Fascist, and nationalistic."[37]

Capitalizing on EU resentment, nationalist and populist parties won elections across Europe. On the right, the Alternative for Germany party won 94 seats in the Bundestag in September 2017; the Freedom Party of Austria joined the governing coalition in October 2017; and conservative, nationalist parties have assumed office in Poland, the Czech Republic, and Hungary.[38] Europe has also seen a resurgence of the far left. In Greece, the Coalition of the Radical Left (Syriza) took power in September 2015; in Portugal, the Left Bloc and Communist party formed an alliance with the Socialist government in November 2015; and in the UK, far-left socialist Jeremy Corbyn took leadership of the UK Labour Party in September 2015.[39] Although the agendas of these parties differ, they share a dislike of the EU and favor a return of state power.

These parties have had significant impact on European politics. Most visibly, the far-right UK Independence Party pushed a popular referendum that resulted in 2016 in the UK exiting the EU, colloqui-

---

[35] Interviews with German government officials and German think tank, Berlin, April 20, 2018.

[36] Krisztina Than and Gabriela Baczynska, "Eastern EU States Tell Brussels to Back Off," Reuters, January 26, 2018; David Herszenhorn and Maia de la Baume, "Juncker and Selmayr Fight Timmermans on Behalf of Poland," *Politico*, June 8, 2018.

[37] Interview with Polish think tank, Warsaw, April 23, 2018.

[38] William A. Galston, "The Rise of European Populism and the Collapse of the Center-Left," Brookings, news blog, March 8, 2018.

[39] Luke March, "2016: The Ebbing of Europe's Radical Left Tide?" *European Futures*, blog post, Edinburgh Europa Institute, November 7, 2016; Axel Bugge, "As Europe Left Struggles, Portugal's Alliance Wins Over Voters and Brussels," Reuters, March 31, 2017; Sheri Berman, "Populism Is a Problem. Elitist Technocrats Aren't the Solution," *Foreign Policy*, December 20, 2017; Antonis Samaras, "Syriza Is Undermining Democracy in Greece," *Financial Times*, March 8, 2018.

ally termed Brexit. Despite suffering in the polls and from internal disputes after the referendum, the party is once again gaining support.[40]

Revanchist Russia

Finally, Europe is divided on how to deal with a revanchist Russia. Although Poland, Ukraine, and the Baltic states have reduced their dependency on Russian energy, Germany plans to construct the Nord Stream 2 pipeline that will transport natural gas directly from Russia to Germany.[41] France relies on Russia for defense contracts, and the British economy is flush with Russian capital.[42] Ideologically, the Baltic states and Poland are diametrically opposed to Putin's Russia while such countries as Italy, Austria, Hungary, and the Czech Republic have pro-Russian factions within their populations and governments.[43]

Consequently, the EU remains conflicted on how to handle Russia. For example, the UK levied several diplomatic punitive measures against Russia in response to the nerve agent attack on Russian spy Sergei Skripal but did not call for additional economic sanctions.[44] For her part, Merkel maintained a tough rhetorical stance on Putin and decided to expel four Russian diplomats from Germany after the

---

[40] Matthew Goodwin, "Ukip Is Back Thanks to the Chequers Backlash," *Spectator*, July 28, 2018.

[41] Chi-Kong Chyong, Louisa Slavkova, and Vessela Tcherneva, "EU Alternatives to Russian Gas," European Council on Foreign Relations, April 9, 2015; Judy Dempsey, "Germany, Dump Nord Stream 2," *Judy Dempsey's Strategic Europe*, Carnegie Europe blog, January 25, 2016; Maciej Martewicz, "Poland Waves Goodbye to Russian Gas After 74 Years," Bloomberg, February 8, 2018; Andrew Rettman, "Germany Starts to Build Nord Stream 2," *EU Observer*, May 4, 2018b.

[42] Bremmer, 2016; interview with British firm, London, April 17, 2018.

[43] Piotr Buras and Adam Balcer, "An Unpredictable Russia: The Impact on Poland," European Council on Foreign Relations, July 15, 2016; Lili Bayer, "Poland and Hungary Stand United (Except on Russia)," *Politico*, September 22, 2017; Gustav Gressel, "Austria: Russia's Trojan Horse?" European Council on Foreign Relations, December 21, 2017; interview with German think tank, Berlin, April 20, 2018.

[44] Emile Simpson, "Theresa May Should Go After Putin's Debt," *Foreign Policy*, March 21, 2018.

Skripal poisoning, yet the Nord Stream 2 project was approved.[45] And ten EU countries—including Austria, Belgium, and Greece—declined to expel any Russian diplomats in response to the attack, illustrating the reluctance of some EU members to poke the proverbial bear.[46]

Future Projection: Increasingly Destabilized, Divided, and Inward-Looking Europe

Looking to 2030, Europe will likely become increasingly divided and grow more inward-looking. Despite the recent decline in migration, migrants will continue to be drawn to Europe, and human smugglers—who have profited from the crisis—will be there to facilitate their travel.[47] Moreover, even if illegal migration were to stop, the EU still needs to contend with the millions of migrants already within its borders, ensuring that the crisis will continue for years to come.

Additionally, Europe remains vulnerable to terrorist attacks. Several studies predict that terrorism will probably increase over the next five to ten years as ISIS's so-called "caliphate" collapses, fighters return home to Europe, and individuals currently imprisoned on material support charges are released between 2019 and 2023.[48] Furthermore, as long as the Schengen Area exists, Europe will continue to face challenges monitoring cross-border terrorist movements.

---

[45] Richard Fuchs, "Germany's Russian Energy Dilemma," *Deutsche Welle*, March 29, 2014; Anca Gurzu, "Germany's Double Gas Game with Russia," *Politico*, March 28, 2018; Andrew Rettman, "Merkel: Nord Stream 2 Is 'Political,'" *EU Observer*, April 11, 2018a.

[46] Leonid Bershidsky, "Europe's Anti-Kremlin Roll Call Was Weak," Bloomberg, March 27, 2018a.

[47] European Union Agency for Law Enforcement Cooperation, *European Union Serious and Organised Crime Assessment 2017*, The Hague, 2017, p. 11; Gabriela Baczynska, "Pressure on EU's Southern Borders from African Migrants Seen Persisting in 2018," Reuters, February 20, 2018.

[48] Office of the Director of National Intelligence, "Paradox of Progress, Near Future: Tensions Are Rising, Growing Terrorism Threat," *Global Trends Main Report*, undated; Jane's IHS Markit, "Terror Risks in Europe to Increase in 2018 as Islamic State's Foreign Fighters Return," press release, February 13, 2018.

Since the rise of identity politics is closely intertwined with the migration crisis and terrorism, support for nationalist and populist parties will likely continue and possibly grow, exploiting the EU's failure to respond to these crises.[49] Such movements could prompt more countries to leave the EU, especially in the aftermath of Brexit. Although Brexit has yet to spur a domino effect across Europe, other countries still might follow Britain's lead. For example, growing tension between the Polish government and the EU Commission has prompted discussion of a referendum on whether Poland should leave the EU, though popular support for this idea is currently very low.[50]

Finally, as mentioned earlier, Russia seems poised to grow more aggressive, not less so, in the years to come. The net result is that causes for schisms within Europe seem poised to persist and possibly intensify over the next decade.

Implications for the U.S. Air Force and the Future of Warfare

The trend toward an increasingly divided and inward-looking Europe holds several implications for the future of warfare and for the joint force. Although NATO will likely continue to remain the cornerstone of European security, if for no other reason than Europe lacks a viable alternative to the U.S.-led alliance, the divisions within Europe provide Russia with an opportunity to constrain the EU and NATO's ability to respond in emergencies, create further instability in Europe, and strain the transatlantic alliance.[51]

---

[49] Lilly Bilyana and Jeremy Shapiro, "Sovereignty's Revenge: The Power of Populism in the European Union," Washington, D.C., Brookings Institution, April 30, 2015.

[50] David M. Herszenhorn, "Warsaw to Trump: Let's Make a Military Deal (Without NATO)," *Politico*, May 30, 2018; "Flirting with Polexit? Poland's President Wants a Referendum on the EU: Most Poles Are Keen to Stay," *The Economist*, June 20, 2018; Jonathan Eyal, "The Other Europe? How Central Europe Views the Continent's Security Concerns and Aspirations," *RUSI Newsbrief*, Vol. 38, No. 5, June 25, 2018.

[51] "In Austria, Russia Hopes to Exploit Europe's Divisions," Stratfor, June 23, 2014; Fiona Hill, "This Is What Putin Really Wants," Washington, D.C., Brookings Institution, Feb-

Europe likely also will become more selective about participating in future expeditionary missions, instead allocating its limited defense resources to more-immediate problems, such as combating terrorism within its borders or defending against Russia.[52] Europe as a whole does not view China as a security threat, so NATO might be unlikely to support any contingency in Asia.[53] Additionally, many European defense experts suggested that NATO's appetite for out-of-area counterterrorism operations might decrease.[54] In the event of another conflict in the Middle East or Asia, the United States might have to call upon an ad hoc coalition of individual allies rather than relying on its usual European allies or the support of NATO as a whole. In this sense, NATO's engagement in Afghanistan, far from Europe's borders, might be the anomaly and the alliance might be likely to return to its more continental focus.

At the national level, the U.S. core European allies will likely remain the same although there will be relative shifts in the strength of each alliance. Table 6.1 lists all the NATO allies with militaries that have more than than 100,000 active personnel. Of all the countries examined, Greece spends the highest percentage of its GDP on defense but is also among the hardest hit by the Eurozone and migrant crises, and it has the lowest opinion of NATO. Italy and Spain face similar economic and migration-related problems and fall far short of meeting

---

ruary 24, 2015; Mark Galeotti, *Controlling Chaos: How Russia Manages Its Political War in Europe*, London: European Council on Foreign Relations, September 1, 2017; Witold Rodkiewicz, "The Russian Attack on the United Kingdom: The Aims and Consequences," Warsaw, OSW Centre for Easter Studies, March 14, 2018; interview with British firm, London, April 16, 2018; interviews with Polish government officials, Warsaw, April 23, 2018; interview with Polish think tank, Warsaw, April 23, 2018.

52 Claudia Major and Christian Molling, "The Framework Nations Concept," *SWP Comments*, No. 52, December 2014, p. 1; NATO, "Defence Expenditure of NATO Countries (2010–2017)," press release 111, June 29, 2017, p. 3.

53 Interview with British think tank, London, April 17, 2018; interviews with NATO officials, Brussels, April 18, 2018; interviews with German government officials, Berlin, April 20, 2018; interviews with Polish government officials, Warsaw, April 23, 2018.

54 Interview with British think tank, London, April 17, 2018; interviews with NATO officials, Brussels, April 18, 2018; interviews with German government officials, Berlin, April 20, 2018; interviews with Polish government officials, Warsaw, April 23, 2018.

NATO's guideline of spending 2 percent of GDP on defense—a target they have indicated they still will not meet by 2024.[55]

Of the four remaining countries, Poland could become the strongest, most dependable European ally, at least regarding Russia. The Polish public overwhelmingly supports defending a NATO ally against Russia, and Poland is one of the top five contributors to NATO in terms of defense expenditure as a share of GDP and becoming increasingly militarily capable.[56] Finally, Poland has the most favorable views of the United States and NATO out of any country in Europe and even offered to finance the construction of a permanent U.S. base in Poland.[57]

Depending on the mission, France also could become a more important ally for the United States. Despite its opposition to the Iraq War, France fought in Afghanistan and Libya and has a vested interest in the global counterterrorism campaign, particularly against ISIS in the Middle East and al Qaeda in the Islamic Maghreb in Africa.[58] Although falling below NATO's defense spending benchmark of 2 percent of GDP, France by many estimates retains one of the largest and best equipped militaries in Europe.[59]

---

[55] DPA and Reuters, "NATO Says More Members Plan to Reach Spending Goal by 2024," Radio Free Europe, February 14, 2018.

[56] "Poland About to Increase Its Defence Expenditure up to the Level of 2.5% of GDP: A New Bill Introduced," Defence24.com, April 24, 2017; NATO, June 29, 2017, p. 3; "Poland Will Increase the Size of Its Military by over 50%," *Global Security Review*, November 16, 2017.

[57] Jaroslaw Adamowski, "Poland Offers up to $2 Billion for a Permanent US Military Presence," *Defense News*, May 29, 2018; Charlie Gao, "Poland Wants Lots of U.S. Military Gear; The Reason: Russia," *National Interest*, June 30, 2018.

[58] Jean-Baptiste Jeangene Vilmer and Olivier Schmitt, "Frogs of War: Explaining the New French Military Interventionism," *War on the Rocks*, October 4, 2015.

[59] Geoffroy Clavel, "France Supports Decision to Stay out of Iraq, but Doesn't Rule Out Future Conflicts," *Huffington Post*, March 19, 2013; Vilmer and Schmitt, 2015; NATO, June 29, 2017, pp. 3, 6.

Table 6.1
Indicators of Alliance Strength

Country	Percentage of Population with Favorable Opinion of the United States	Percentage of Population That Would Fight to Defend Their Country	Percentage of Population in Favor of Defending NATO Allies Against Russia	Percentage of Population with Favorable Opinion of NATO	Defense Expenditure as Percentage of GDP	Defense Expenditure in Millions of U.S. Dollars	Number of Active Military Personnel
Poland	73	47	62	79	1.99	10,654	111,000
Germany	35	18	40	67	1.24	47,458	180,000
UK	50	27	45	62	2.12	56,993	161,000
France	46	29	53	60	1.79	47,933	209,000
Italy	61	20	Unavailable	57	1.12	24,390	181,000
Spain	31	21	46	45	0.92	12,600	121,000
Greece	43	54	Unavailable	33	2.36	4,943	106,000

SOURCE: Worldwide Independent Network/Gallup International, "WIN/Gallup International's Global Survey Shows Three in Five Willing to Fight for Their Country," webpage, 2015; Pew Research Center, "Global Indicators Database: Opinion of the United States—Do You Have a Favorable or Unfavorable View of the U.S.?" webpage, Spring 2017; "Germans Least Supportive of Defending Allies Against Russia," webpage, Pew Research Center, May 22, 2017.
NOTE: Defense expenditure figures were converted from national currency units to U.S. dollars using the exchange rate as of July 10, 2018, and rounded to the nearest whole number.

Going forward, the UK might show less willingness to engage in expeditionary operations.[60] As a House of Commons report noted, "The sensitivity of public opinion to military casualties incurred in wars perceived to have no clear purpose or definition of victory, together with constraints on public spending, mean the threshold for future interventions will be high."[61] Nonetheless, the UK still supported the United States in the April 2018 Syria strikes in suggesting, despite public backlash, that it will remain a close, if more restrained, U.S. ally.[62] Post-Brexit, the UK could even increase its commitment to NATO as that becomes the UK's primary format for security cooperation with European allies.[63]

Finally, Germany will likely become a more reluctant and less reliable partner for the United States.[64] In theory, Germany has resources to be the cornerstone of European security and the transatlantic alliance, but in practice, this remains unlikely. Although Germans are supportive of NATO in the abstract, they are among the least support-

---

[60] Worldwide Independent Network/Gallup International, 2015; Rachael Gribble, Simon Wessley, Susan Klein, David A. Alexander, Christopher Dandeker, and Nicola T. Fear, "British Public Opinion After a Decade of War: Attitudes to Iraq and Afghanistan," *Politics: 2014*, Vol. 35, No. 2, 2015; interviews with British government officials, London, April 16, 2018; interview with British think tank, London, April 17, 2018.

[61] Gavin Thompson, Oliver Hawkins, Aliyah Dar, Mark Taylor, Nick Battley, Adam Mellows-Facer, Chris Rhodes, Daniel Harari, Dominic Webb, Feargal McGuinness, Gavin Berman, Grahame Allen, Lorna Booth, Lucinda Maer, Matthew Keep, Nida Broughton, Paul Bolton, Rachael Harker, Richard Cracknell, Roderick McInnes, and Tom Rutherford, *Olympic Britain: Social and Economic Change Since the 1908 and 1948 London Games*, London: House of Commons Publications, 2012, pp. 155–156.

[62] Pierre Tran and Andrew Chuter, "Domestic Response to Syria Strikes: Cheers in France, Lashing in UK," *Defense News*, April 16, 2018.

[63] James Black, Alexandra Hall, Kate Cox, Marta Kepe, and Erik Silfversten, *Defence and Security After Brexit: Understanding the Possible Implications of the UK's Decision to Leave the EU—Overview Report*, Santa Monica, Calif.: RAND Corporation, RR-1786/1-RC, 2017, p. 11.

[64] Interview with German think tank, Berlin, April 20, 2018. See Christopher Alessi, "How Afghanistan Changed the German Military," *Spiegel Online*, October 15, 2013; and Rick Noack, "Afraid of a Major Conflict? The German Military Is Currently Unavailable," *Washington Post*, January 24, 2018.

ive of defending a NATO ally against Russia.[65] Even if the will to fight existed, Germany's Bundeswehr faces serious equipment shortages and German defense spending will remain far below NATO guidelines for the foreseeable future.[66] All that aside, Germany's historical past and its present-day tension with other European countries over immigration, economic policy, and other issues pose obstacles to the idea of it leading Europe on the security front.

---

65 "Germans Least Supportive of Defending Allies Against Russia," 2017.

66 Konstantin von Hammerstein and Peter Muller, "U.S. Pressures Germany to Increase Defense Spending," *Spiegel Online*, February 17, 2017; Elisabeth Braw, "Germany Is Quietly Building a European Army Under Its Command," *Foreign Affairs*, May 22, 2017a; NATO, June 29, 2017, p. 3; Elisabeth Braw, "Europe's Readiness Problem," *Foreign Affairs*, November 30, 2017b; Andrea Shalal, "Equipment Shortages Impair German Military Ahead of Key NATO Mission," Reuters, February 19, 2018; Leonid Bershidsky, "The U.S. Should Move Troops from Germany to Poland," Bloomberg, May 30, 2018b.

CHAPTER SEVEN

Trend 6: Turmoil in the Islamic World

Although China and Russia arguably pose a greater strategic threat, U.S. wars since at least the September 11, 2001, terrorist attacks have focused on three interconnected challenges emanating from the Islamic world—terrorism, instability, and simmering interstate tension.[1] Looking out to 2030, these three challenges will continue to shape the future of warfare and drive U.S. military commitments.

Context: Sectarian and Ethnic Conflict Occurs After Authoritarian Collapse

Scholarship points to at least two fundamental insights in understanding the turmoil afflicting the Islamic world. First, although scholars are divided about drivers of Islamic terrorism, few say they believe that any of these underlying causes—whether they are economic opportunity, social mobility, political inclusiveness, or simple religious fervor—have been addressed.[2] Second, democratic transitions after authoritarian collapse—such as occurred during the Arab Spring—often go awry

[1] This report defines the Islamic world as the Middle East, North Africa, Afghanistan, and Pakistan.

[2] For a sample of the debate over the causes of terrorism, see Jennifer L. Windsor, "Promoting Democratization Can Combat Terrorism," *Washington Quarterly*, Vol. 26, No. 3, 2003; James A. Piazza, "Draining the Swamp: Democracy Promotion, State Failure, and Terrorism in 19 Middle Eastern Countries," *Studies in Conflict & Terrorism*, Vol. 30, No. 6, 2007; and Mark Juergensmeyer, *Terror in the Mind of God: The Global Rise of Religious Violence*, 4th ed., Oakland, Calif.: University of California Press, 2017.

and can produce protracted domestic conflict, particularly if they occur suddenly and threaten to upend social and political order.[3] Taken together, both findings suggest that turmoil in the Middle East will likely continue for some time to come.

Historical Trend: Descent into Chaos

For decades, powerful, if brutal, strongmen ruled much of the Islamic world. Former military officers governed Yemen, Egypt, Libya, Iraq, and Tunisia. In some countries—such as Syria, Jordan, and Saudi Arabia—power became institutionalized under a monarchy or hereditary authoritarian rule. The exception was the Islamic Republic of Iran, which had a severely limited democracy under tight control of the clerics. Despite a series of interstate wars (the Iran-Iraq War, Gulf War, or the multiple Arab-Israeli conflicts), the countries themselves remained internally stable.

A series of events caused this fragile stability to unravel, however. In 2001, al Qaeda successfully carried out the September 11 terrorist attacks, prompting the U.S. invasion of Afghanistan and the start of the Global War on Terrorism. Two years later, in 2003, the United States invaded Iraq and toppled the first of the region's longtime strongmen, Saddam Hussein, thereby removing the greatest regional counterweight to Iran. Arguably, a far greater blow to regional stability came during the 2011 Arab Spring, when popular protests toppled other strongmen in Tunisia, Libya, Yemen, and Egypt, and sparked violence in Syria, Bahrain, and elsewhere.

Even in 2018, chaos still consumes much of the region. According to Chairman of the Joint Chiefs of Staff General Joseph Dunford, the

---

[3] For the classic argument about democratic revolutions and war, see Edward D. Mansfield and Jack Snyder, *Electing to Fight: Why Emerging Democracies Go to War*, Cambridge, Mass.: MIT Press, 2005. For some attempts to explain this in the context of Arab world, see Jason Brownlee, Tarek Masoud, and Andrew Reynolds, "Why the Modest Harvest?" *Journal of Democracy*, Vol. 24, No. 4, October 2013; and Nathan Brown, "Egypt's Failed Transition," *Journal of Democracy*, Vol. 24, No. 4, October 2013.

Afghanistan war remains "roughly a stalemate."[4] In Syria and Yemen, civil wars continue and there is little prospect for returning to a stable, centralized government in either country.[5] In Libya, rival militias vie for power.[6] Outside the active war zones, experts argue that popular discontent is often simmering just below the surface and ready to erupt even in such seemingly peaceful places as Algeria, Tunisia, Egypt, and Jordan.[7]

Over the past decade and a half, internal instability allowed Islamic terrorism to thrive. In the unrest that followed the invasion, Iraq became a breeding ground for local insurgents unhappy with changes in power and later a magnet for foreign Islamic terrorists as well, including members of al Qaeda. Islamic terrorist groups also found homes in other weak states, such as Afghanistan, Somalia, Yemen, or Libya after Qaddafi's regime toppled. More recently, ISIS capitalized on the chaos left by the Arab Spring and seized vast swathes of Syria and Iraq. Although many of these territorial gains have since been reversed, ISIS and radical Islamic terrorism more broadly continues to exist.

The regional chaos also exacerbated a sectarian-infused interstate competition, primarily between Iran and Saudi Arabia, for who will control the Middle East. Instability in primarily Sunni-led regimes presented an opportunity for Iran to expand what it sees as its rightful sphere of regional influence, including into its former

---

[4] Kenneth Katzman and Clayton Thomas, *Afghanistan: Post-Taliban Governance, Security and U.S. Policy*, Washington, D.C.: Congressional Research Service, RL30588, November 7, 2017, pp. 26, 53.

[5] Carla E. Humud, Christopher M. Blanchard, and Mary Beth D. Nikitin, *Armed Conflict in Syria: Overview and U.S. Response*, Washington, D.C.: Congressional Research Service, RL33487, October 13, 2017, p. 40.

[6] Elissa Miller and Kevin Truitte, "Filling the Vacuum in Libya," *Foreign Affairs*, July 18, 2017.

[7] Francisco Serrano, "Algeria on the Brink? Five Years After the Arab Spring," *Foreign Affairs*, May 27, 2017; Sarah E. Yerkes, "Democracy Derailed? Tunisia's Transition Veers Off Course," *Foreign Affairs*, October 2, 2017; Alexia Underwood, "Sisi Won Egypt's Election. That Doesn't Mean He's Safe," Vox.com, April 3, 2018; interview with Jordanian think tank, Amman, May 12–13, 2018.

adversaries, such as Iraq.[8] In the zero-sum politics of the Middle East, what Iran saw as an opportunity, Saudi Arabia saw a mortal threat. As Professor F. Gregory Gause notes, "The Arab Spring only heightened Riyadh's sense of encirclement," as primarily Sunni-led, Saudi-allied regimes fell.[9]

The simmering conflict between Iran and Saudi Arabia has taken on many forms. In Lebanon, Saudi Arabia forced the resignation of Prime Minister Saad Hariri in November 2017 after he did not crack down on Iran's premier proxy force, Hezbollah.[10] In other cases, the competition has turned violent. In Syria, the Iranian Revolutionary Guard Corps provided military assistance and funding—estimated at between $6 billion and $20 billion annually—to the Assad regime while Saudi Arabia reportedly funded the opposition.[11] The sides are also locked in an increasingly bloody proxy war in Yemen between the Saudi Arabia–backed Yemeni government and the Iranian-backed Shiite Houthi rebels.[12] The Iran-Saudi conflict reaches beyond the Persian Gulf and threatens to engulf much of the Islamic world: States from Morocco to Afghanistan have needed to pick sides.[13]

---

[8] Kenneth Katzman, *Iran's Foreign and Defense Policies*, Washington, D.C.: Congressional Research Service, R44017, November 7, 2017, p. 2.

[9] F. Gregory Gause III, "The Future of U.S. Saudi Relations: The Kingdom and the Power," *Foreign Affairs*, June 13, 2016.

[10] Bilal Y. Saab, "Don't Let the Saudis Destabilize Lebanon: Why Washington Should Restrain Riyadh," *Foreign Affairs*, November 20, 2017.

[11] Mark Mazzetti and Matt Apuzzo, "U.S. Relies Heavily on Saudi Money to Support Syrian Rebels," *New York Times*, January 23, 2016; Katzman, 2017, p. 34; Alex Vatanka, "Iran and Russia, Growing Apart: Rising Dissent over the IRGC's Militias," *Foreign Affairs*, November 29, 2017.

[12] David D. Kirkpatrick, "Saudi Arabia Charges Iran with 'Act of War,' Raising Threat of Military Clash," *New York Times*, November 6, 2017.

[13] Payam Mohseni and Hussein Kalout, "Iran's Axis of Resistance Rises: How It's Forging a New Middle East," *Foreign Affairs*, October 23, 2017.

Future Projection: Terrorism, Instability, and Regional Conflict

There is little evidence to suggest that the turmoil roiling the Islamic world will resolve itself over the next ten to 15 years. To the contrary, there are several good reasons to believe that these challenges will continue and perhaps even intensify over the next decade. Thus, the U.S. military should expect similar, or perhaps increased, demand for resources to address these problems.

Continued Radical Islamic Terrorism

Despite recent successes in the war on terrorism, there are three reasons that the United States will probably still face an ongoing threat for the next decade from radical Islamic terrorist groups in the Islamic world. First, as terrorism expert Seth Jones remarks, Islamic terrorist groups' strength have "never been linear, but [have] waxed and waned based on such factors as the collapse of governments in countries such as Iraq, Syria, and Yemen."[14] Jones further notes that any number of factors could lead to rebirth of the movement, such as withdrawal of U.S. military presence, another Arab Spring, or a new charismatic leader.[15]

Moreover, although the United States notched victories against ISIS, Shiite terrorist groups have grown increasingly capable. Lebanese Hezbollah now numbers some 40,000 troops, many of whom have recent combat experience in Syria.[16] Thanks to an estimated $100–$200 million in Iranian funding, the group has amassed an arsenal of 150,000 rockets, Russian-made SA-22 missiles, drones, and other advanced military capabilities.[17] Although perhaps less capable, Iraq's Shiite militias are more numerous, with between 110,000 and 120,000

---

[14] Seth G. Jones, "Will al Qaeda Make a Comeback? The Factors That Will Determine Its Success," *Foreign Affairs*, August 7, 2017.

[15] Jones, 2017.

[16] Jonathan Schanzer, "The Iran Deal's Bigger Loser: Hezbollah's Uncertain Future," *Foreign Affairs*, March 20, 2016.

[17] Schanzer, 2016.

troops.[18] These groups—such as Asa'ib Ahl al-Haq (League of the Family of the Righteous) or Kata'ib Hezbollah (Hezbollah Battalions)—are also allegedly backed by Iran and have attacked U.S. forces in the past.[19]

Finally, even if the United States successfully eliminated both Sunni and Shiite Islamic terrorism in the Middle East, that still might not put an end to the threat. Radical Islamic terrorist groups now span the globe from Libya to Nigeria; Mali to Somalia; across Central Asia; through Afghanistan and Pakistan; and into Southeast Asia, particularly the Philippines, Malaysia, and Indonesia—not to mention offshoots operating in the West.[20] Consequently, it is unlikely that the United States and its allies will decisively eliminate radical Islamic terrorism by 2030.

Ongoing Internal Instability

Rooting out terrorism will be made more complex by the ongoing problem of internal instability that will almost certainly plague the region through 2030. As already noted, few of the Islamic world's current conflicts appear to be nearing a permanent resolution. Even in the handful of countries where the violence has subsided, such as Iraq, bitterness and distrust between the factions remains largely unaddressed and could easily slide into open conflict.[21]

Furthermore, if the ongoing conflicts in the Islamic world were to end tomorrow, the sheer scale of existing damage would leave these countries prone to instability for some time to come. For example, Afghanistan's decades of conflict have left 2 million dead and millions more wounded or displaced.[22] Similarly, Syria's prewar population was

---

[18] Kenneth Katzman and Carla E. Humud, *Iraq: Politics and Governance*, Washington, D.C., Congressional Research Service, RS21960, March 9, 2016, p. 17.

[19] Katzman and Humud, 2016, p. 18.

[20] The UK, for example, announced that it was tracking 23,000 "subjects of interest" alone. "23,000 People Have Been 'Subjects of Interest' as Scale of Terror Threat Emerges After Manchester Attack," *Telegraph*, May 27, 2017.

[21] Emma Sky, "Mission Still Not Accomplished in Iraq: Why the United States Should Not Leave," *Foreign Affairs*, October 16, 2017.

[22] Katzman and Thomas, 2017, pp. 26, 53.

22 million; hundreds of thousands are now dead, many more wounded, and almost half that prewar number is believed to be internally displaced or living abroad as refugees.[23] Unsurprisingly, experts predict that restoring regional stability will take years—perhaps decades.[24]

In addition, the ongoing instability might yet spread to other neighboring countries, any of which could erupt in violence between now and 2030. Jordan, for example, is home to Palestinian, Iraqi, and now Syrian refugees—the Syrian population alone numbers 1.4 million in a country of 7.5 million—contributing to an unemployment rate of 22 percent and increasing pressure on the ruling monarchy.[25] Similar to Jordan, Lebanon shelters some 1.5 million Syrian refugees and is still dealing with the effects of its own civil war and wars with Israel, most recently in 2006.[26]

Finally, the region's other strongmen might still fall. Saudi Arabia's young Crown Prince Mohammed bin Salman is trying to consolidate power to reform the conservative Saudi state, earning plaudits from abroad but risking a backlash from the powerful conservative elements within Saudi society and elsewhere in the royal family.[27] Similarly, although military leader Abed Fattah el-Sisi has consolidated his control over Egypt for the moment, the country still faces a host of economic and terrorism problems, and the popular discontent that resulted in the overthrow of his predecessor remains.[28] Turkish President Recep Tayyip Erdoğan's regime already faced one failed military coup in July 2016; the response was to arrest 60,000 people and fire

---

[23] Humud, Blanchard, and Nikitin, 2017, p. i.

[24] Interviews with Jordanian academics and think tank officials, Amman, May 12–13, 2018.

[25] Rana F. Sweis, "Jordan Struggles Under a Wave of Syrian Refugees," *New York Times*, February 13, 2016; Interviews with Jordanian academics and think tank officials, Amman, May 12–13, 2018.

[26] Saab, 2017.

[27] Interviews with Israeli academics, Tel Aviv, May 8–10, 2018; interviews with Jordanian officials, Amman, May 12–13, 2018; interviews with U.S. government officials, Abu Dhabi, May 15, 2018.

[28] Underwood, 2018.

150,000 government employees to try to consolidate power.[29] Given the size and importance of these countries, instability in any of them would have regional consequences.

Intensifying Regional Conflict

It is possible that the greatest concern for the United States and the factor most likely to drive a significant increase in U.S. military presence over the next decade will be neither terrorism nor internal instability but a large-scale regional conflict. Looking to 2030, multiple states in the region will have reasons to escalate the already simmering interstate conflict in the region.

First, with a friendly regime in Iraq, less U.S. conventional presence in the region, and an Assad regime with a firmer grip over Syria, Iran will enjoy a comparatively benign strategic environment and be better positioned than in the past to fulfill its ambitions for regional hegemony.[30] It will likely be able to capitalize on its extensive network of terrorist and militia groups throughout the region that it developed over the past several decades.[31] Iran enjoys an alliance of convenience with Russia, giving it additional great-power cover for its actions. At the same time, Iran will face increasing economic troubles. Despite the Joint Comprehensive Plan of Action and the sanctions relief after the nuclear deal, Iran's economy never fully bounced back, creating popular discontent toward the regime.[32] If the United States successfully reimposes sanctions, this might only increase the pain, potentially strengthening Iran's hard-line political factions and increasing the chances that Iran might use international conflict to divert public attention away from its domestic problems.[33]

---

[29] Jim Zanotti and Clayton Thomas, *Turkey: Background and U.S. Relations in Brief*, Washington, D.C.: Congressional Research Service, R44000, November 9, 2017, pp. 12–14.

[30] Katzman, 2017, p. 21.

[31] Katzman, 2017, pp. 4, 12–13; Vatanka, 2017.

[32] Ladane Nasseri, Golnar Motevalli, and Arsalan Shahla, "After Sanctions, Iran's Economy Is Nearing a Crisis," Bloomberg, August 9, 2018.

[33] Nasseri, Motevalli, and Shahla, 2018.

Second, Saudi Arabia will likely feel increasingly insecure. Given its growing internal problems—such as low oil prices, radicalization, and terrorism—Saudi Arabia might become increasingly sensitive to any real or perceived Iranian threats to its stability or its fellow Sunni regimes.[34] Moreover, aggressive pushback against expanding Iranian interests could also serve the royal family's domestic political interests, helping bin Salman consolidate his power and advance his domestic agenda.

Third, other Sunni Arab states will view growing Iranian influence with apprehension and might become increasingly concerned that Iran will provoke unrest in their Shiite minorities.[35] Although these states might not want war per se, they have already demonstrated that they will follow Saudi Arabia's lead. In 2015, Saudi Arabia assembled a coalition that included support from not only the Gulf States but also Egypt, Jordan, and even Sudan to intervene against Iranian-backed rebels in the Yemeni civil war.[36] Years later, many of these states continue to fight in Yemen, even if they privately doubt the wisdom of such actions.[37] More recently, Bahrain, Egypt, and the United Arab Emirates joined the Saudi Arabia–led boycott of Qatar in June 2017 that was ostensibly for supporting terrorist groups (such as Hamas) but was also in retaliation for Qatar's close relationship with Iran.[38]

Israel has its own reasons to fight. Like the Sunni Arab states, Israel has expressed alarm at Tehran's growing regional influence and views Iranian military presence in Syria as a redline.[39] Israel also views

---

[34] Christopher M. Blanchard, *Saudi Arabia: Background and U.S. Relations*, Washington, D.C.: Congressional Research Service, CL33533, November 22, 2017, pp. 1, 9, 14–15.

[35] Interviews with Jordanian officials, Amman, May 12–13, 2018; interviews with U.S. officials, Abu Dhabi, May 15, 2018.

[36] Reuters, "Which Countries Are Part of Saudi Arabia's Coalition Against Yemen's Houthis?" *Huffington Post*, March 26, 2015.

[37] Interviews with Jordanian officials, Amman, May 12–13, 2018; interviews with U.S. officials, Abu Dhabi, May 15, 2018.

[38] Bassima Alghussein and Jeffrey A. Stacey, "How Saudi Arabia Botched Its Campaign Against Qatar: The Cost of the Pressure on Doha," *Foreign Affairs*, July 12, 2017.

[39] Interviews with Israeli academics, Tel Aviv, May 8–10, 2018.

Iranian nuclear weapons as an existential threat and has always doubted Iran's promises to denuclearize;[40] it already has struck Iranian targets in Syria, but Iran seems unlikely to abandon its military foothold there.[41] Moreover, with the U.S. withdrawal from the Joint Comprehensive Plan of Action, Iran could restart its nuclear program. Even if Iran remained in compliance for a short time to avoid angering the other signatories, many of the restrictions on its nuclear program that were included in the Joint Comprehensive Plan of Action were set to expire by 2030, meaning that Iran could resume some nuclear-related activities.[42] Were that to happen, the chances of a large scale Israeli-Iranian confrontation by 2030 would increase substantially.

Finally, as mentioned earlier, with its intervention in Syria, Russia also has increased its military presence in the Middle East. With other great powers—notably China—dependent on the region for energy, the Middle East could very well be at the epicenter of future great-power competition.[43]

Implications for the U.S. Air Force and the Future of Warfare

The real question might not be whether the Islamic world will remain afflicted by terrorism, instability, and intensifying conflict through 2030. Rather the question might be to what extent the United States will choose to fight these wars, particularly as it becomes less reliant on

---

[40] Isabel Kershner and Thomas Erdbrink, "As Deadline on Nuclear Deal Nears, Israel and Iran Issue Warnings," *New York Times*, May 6, 2018.

[41] Amos Harel, "Israel Signals Lull in Syria Strikes Is Over, Resuming Military Action Against Iran," *Ha'aretz*, September 5, 2018.

[42] China, France, Germany, European Union, Iran, Russia, United Kingdom, and United States, Joint Comprehensive Plan of Action, Vienna, July 14, 2015.

[43] In 2017, China imported 56 percent of its oil from the Organization of Petroleum Exporting Countries, including sizable quantities from Saudi Arabia, Oman, and other Middle Eastern members of the cartel. Holly Ellyatt, "China's Slowing Demand for Oil Is a Serious Concern for the Middle East," CNBC, September 3, 2018.

the region for energy.[44] As mentioned in Chapter Two, popular opinion likely will not support a large-scale military intervention (especially in the Middle East). But the United States has already learned that extricating itself from the region is easier said than done. At the very least, the United States will likely be forced to maintain a robust counterterrorism force to check the global jihadist movement and prevent future attacks on Americans and U.S. soil.

Still, it is possible that U.S. involvement might need to go beyond counterterrorism. As already discussed, the problems of internal instability, regional conflict, and international terrorism are intertwined. If the United States wants to get at these underlying problems, it will need to expand its involvement. Moreover, if the turmoil affecting much of the Islamic world spirals from being a "local" problem into a broader regional war, the United States might find itself forced to act both to stabilize the region and to protect its key allies there. Finally, the United States could find itself in the Middle East for reasons quite apart from regional dynamics altogether: as part of the broader great-power competition with Russia and China.

From the USAF-specific perspective, this analysis has important implications for force planning and budgetary considerations. The service currently remains at the forefront of the counterterrorism effort—providing intelligence, surveillance, and reconnaissance and strike support—and these missions will probably continue going forward. This, in turn, will make it difficult for civilian policymakers and the USAF to swing resources away from the Middle East to Europe or Asia without incurring additional risk on the counterterrorism front.

---

[44] Overall U.S. oil imports already were expected to fall in 2018 to their lowest levels in 60 years, and Persian Gulf countries supplied only 17 percent of what the United States did import. Alan Neuhauser, "EIA: U.S. Net Oil Imports to Drop to Lowest Levels in 60 Years," *US News*, July 18, 2018; U.S. Energy Information Agency, "How Much Petroleum Does the United States Import and Export?" webpage, October 3, 2018.

CHAPTER EIGHT

Conclusions

In the final analysis, all six trends—U.S. polarization and retrenchment, China's rise, Asia's reassessment, a revanchist Russia, upheaval in Europe, and turmoil in the Islamic world—will each shape who, how, where, when, and why the United States will fight through 2030 (Table 8.1). First, at the very least, U.S. polarization and disillusionment will disrupt long-term defense budgeting efforts and could make the use of force an increasingly attractive option for U.S. policymakers, but these factors also could create a vacuum that U.S. adversaries will be able to exploit. Second, China's growing ambitions, rising power, and increasing domestic political pressure could combine to make it more inclined to use force. Third, Asia's strategic reassessment seems poised to change who might join future U.S. military coalitions while also potentially increasing the overall chances of war in Asia, most notably if U.S. allies choose to push back against perceived Chinese encroachment—especially in such disputed areas as Taiwan, the South China Sea, and the Senkaku Islands. Fourth, Russia is increasingly aggressive, especially in its near abroad, both in asserting its own sphere of influence and in defending against perceived Western threats to the regime. Fifth, Europe's attention by contrast is increasingly focused inward on such problems as the migrant crisis, terrorism, and a revanchist Russia, which is sapping Europe's overall will to engage in expeditionary operations and, to some extent, shifting which states are the most militarily dependable U.S. allies. Finally, the turmoil in the Islamic world that has prompted the United States to engage in a sustained counterterrorism effort over the past decade and a

Table 8.1
Summary of Findings

Trend	Who Will Fight	How They Might Fight	Where They Might Fight	When They Might Fight	Why They Might Fight
U.S. polarization and retrenchment	United States	Airpower and special operations forces rather than conventional ground forces			Overconfidence in the military combined with distrust of other tools of national power
China's rise	China and its immediate neighbors	High-end conflict but also measures short of war	Taiwan, South China Sea, Senkaku Islands	If China's economy slows; potentially as Xi's tenure comes to a close	Domestic pressure; expanding strategic periphery
Asia's reassessment	More new partners and allies (e.g., Vietnam/India); less others (e.g., the Philippines)	More maritime conflicts (air-sea cooperation)			Nationalism; fear of rising China
A revanchist Russia	Russia and its neighbors	High-end threat but also measures short of war	Russia's near abroad (but with second-order effects for Asia and the Middle East)		Combination of Russian insecurity and desire for a greater sphere of influence
Upheaval in Europe	More Poland and France; less Germany; more-restrained UK		Eastern Europe (in response to Russian aggression)		Counterterrorism; response to Russian aggression
Turmoil in the Islamic world	Terrorist groups, Arab States, Iran, Israel	Sustained low-level conflict/ counterterrorism	Middle East, North Africa, Central Asia	Now ongoing	Counterterrorism / alliance entrapment

half will likely continue for the next decade and could prompt additional involvement.

Taken together, these trends suggest three overarching implications for the USAF specifically and for the U.S. defense strategy more broadly. First, this analysis validates many of the underlying assumptions in the U.S. *National Defense Strategy*. Great-power competition—specifically with China and Russia—will increasingly define the geopolitical landscape looking forward to 2030.[1] That said, the United States also will need to worry about the other problems posed by Iran, North Korea, and terrorism.[2] As the *National Defense Strategy* implies, the chances of high-end war could increase in the future as the U.S. military advantage shrinks; on the other hand, U.S. adversaries also prefer to achieve their aims short of armed conflict if possible.[3] Finally, as the *National Defense Strategy* indicates, the Indo-Pacific, Europe, and Middle East will probably remain areas where the United States will need to deter aggression.[4]

Second, and on a perhaps deeper level, U.S. alliances will slowly and subtly change. As Asia reassesses its strategic position in response to the rise of China and as Europe combats its own internal challenges, there will be new strategic openings—such as those with Vietnam or India. In other cases, old allies—such as the Philippines—will try to hedge. In still other cases, current allies—such as many of the European partners—will remain firmly pro-American but might lose the will to fight much beyond their own immediate interests. In sum, although it remains unlikely that any one country will terminate its security relationship with the United States, the United States will almost certainly go to war with a very different set of coalition partners in the next war than it has over the past several decades.

Taken together, these geopolitical trends suggest that the United States will face a deepening strategic dilemma regarding how to invest its limited strategic resources in the coming years. Few of the trends

---

1 Department of Defense, 2018, p. 1.

2 Department of Defense, 2018, p. 2.

3 Department of Defense, 2018, p. 3.

4 Department of Defense, 2018, p. 6.

examined here are in the United States' favor; as already noted, there are multiple potential conflicts in the Indo-Pacific, Europe, and the Middle East that could involve the United States. And this is not an exhaustive list: There are other potential black swans not examined here—such as a conflict in Latin America or Africa—that could drive U.S. force commitments. Even if these conflicts do not occur, the United States might be increasingly pressed to extend a credible conventional deterrent to its allies around the globe while avoiding potentially destabilizing vertical or horizontal escalation, particularly if China continues to grow at its current rate.

There is no obvious way to prioritize potential conflicts. A war in the Indo-Pacific with China—the only power that could rival U.S. military capability in 2030—is probably the most dangerous scenario that the United States faces. But it is most likely that the next conflict will be in the Middle East, given that the United States is fighting there currently and the causes of that conflict are unlikely to be resolved any time soon. Ideally, the USAF and the joint force would receive clear, sustained direction from the political leadership about where to place its limited resources, but the polarization of the U.S. electorate suggests that such definitive guidance will not be forthcoming. As a result, defense strategists could find themselves mired in a deepening strategic quandary—with growing threats, limited resources, and little clear guidance about when and where to accept risk.

To be clear, this is not a harbinger of the inevitability of war in 2030. As mentioned in the introduction, war in general has been on the decline when viewed in the grand sweep of history. These trends notwithstanding, there are many reasons—nuclear weapons, trade, and international institutions, to name a few—to believe that great-power conflict will remain a rare occurrence. Nonetheless, if "war is the continuation of politics by other means," as von Clausewitz postulated, then the geopolitical trends do point to darker times ahead.

References

"23,000 People Have Been 'Subjects of Interest' as Scale of Terror Threat Emerges After Manchester Attack," *Telegraph*, May 27, 2017. As of December 13, 2017: http://www.telegraph.co.uk/news/2017/05/27/23000-people-have-subjects-interest-scale-terror-threat-emerges/

Acharya, Amitav, "Will Asia's Past Be Its Future?" *International Security*, Vol. 28, No. 3, Winter 2003/2004, pp. 149–164.

Adamowski, Jaroslaw, "Poland Offers up to $2 Billion for a Permanent US Military Presence," *Defense News*, May 29, 2018. As of July 18, 2018: https://www.defensenews.com/flashpoints/2018/05/29/poland-offers-up-to-2-billion-for-a-permanent-us-military-presence/

Alessi, Christopher, "How Afghanistan Changed the German Military," *Spiegel Online*, October 15, 2013. As of July 18, 2018: http://www.spiegel.de/international/germany/how-afghanistan-has-changed-the-bundeswehr-german-military-a-927891.html

Alghussein, Bassima, and Jeffrey A. Stacey, "How Saudi Arabia Botched Its Campaign Against Qatar: The Cost of the Pressure on Doha," *Foreign Affairs*, July 12, 2017. As of December 6, 2017: https://www.foreignaffairs.com/print/1120463

Allison, Graham, *Destined for War: Can America and China Escape Thucydides's Trap?* Boston: Houghton Mifflin Harcourt, 2017.

Archick, Kristin, *The European Union: Current Challenges and Future Prospects*, Washington, D.C.: Congressional Research Service, R44249, February 27, 2017. As of July 18, 2018: https://fas.org/sgp/crs/row/R44249.pdf

———, *The European Union: Questions and Answers*, Washington, D.C.: Congressional Research Service, RS21372, September 7, 2018. As of October 25, 2018: https://fas.org/sgp/crs/row/RS21372.pdf

"Armeniya ratifitsirovala soglashenie s RF ob ob"edinennoi gruppirovke voisk" ["Armenia Ratified the Agreement with RF on Joint Force"], Interfax.ru, October 5, 2017. As of February 9, 2018:
http://www.interfax.ru/world/581847

Asmus, Ronald, *A Little War That Shook the World: Georgia, Russia, and the Future of the West*, New York: St. Martin's Press, 2010.

Auslin, Michael, "Duterte's Defiance: His Threat to Upend Washington's Pivot to Asia," *Foreign Affairs*, November 2, 2016. As of November 20, 2017:
https://www.foreignaffairs.com/print/1118753

———, *Japanese Internationalism in the 21st Century: Reshaping Foreign Policy in an Era of Upheaval*, Washington, D.C.: American Enterprise Institute, 2017a. As of November 22, 2017:
http://www.aei.org/wp-content/uploads/2017/11/Japanese-Internationalism-in-the-21st-Century.pdf

———, "Can the Doklam Dispute Be Resolved? The Dangers of China and India's Border Standoff," *Foreign Affairs*, August 1, 2017b. As of November 22, 2017:
https://www.foreignaffairs.com/print/1120576

Ayres, Alyssa, "Will India Start Acting Like a Global Power? New Delhi's New Role," *Foreign Affairs*, October 16, 2017. As of November 22, 2017:
https://www.foreignaffairs.com/print/1120974

Ayres, Alyssa, Elizabeth Economy, and Daniel Markey, "Rebalance the Rebalance: China, India, and the United States," *Foreign Affairs*, July 13, 2016. As of November 22, 2017:
https://www.foreignaffairs.com/print/1117829

Babones, Salvatore, "Taipei's Name Game: It's Time to Let Taiwan Be Taiwan," *Foreign Affairs*, December 11, 2016. As of November 15, 2017:
https://www.foreignaffairs.com/articles/taiwan/2016-12-11/taipeis-name-game

Baczynska, Gabriela, "Pressure on EU's Southern Borders from African Migrants Seen Persisting in 2018," Reuters, February 20, 2018. As of July 18, 2018:
https://www.reuters.com/article/us-europe-migrants-eu-frontex/pressure-on-eus-southern-borders-from-african-migrants-seen-persisting-in-2018-idUSKCN1G42AK

Barker, Alex, and James Politi, "Brussels Draws Fire from Rome over Migration Proposals," *Financial Times*, June 20, 2018. As of July 18, 2018:
https://www.ft.com/content/da0189a8-74b6-11e8-aa31-31da4279a601

Barnes, Julian E., "U.S. Seeks Better Deterrence in Europe Against Russian Aircraft," *Wall Street Journal*, April 21, 2016. As of December 5, 2018:
https://www.wsj.com/articles/u-s-seeks-better-deterrence-in-europe-against-russian-aircraft-1461245778?mg=prod/accounts-wsj

Batyrshin, R., "Interv'yu Vladimira Putina teleradiokompanii «Mir»" ["Interview of Vladimir Putin on the Mir TV and Radio Company"], Kremlin.ru, April 12, 2017. As of January 26, 2018:
http://kremlin.ru/events/president/news/54271

Bayer, Lili, "Poland and Hungary Stand United (Except on Russia)," *Politico*, September 22, 2017. As of July 18, 2018:
https://www.politico.eu/article/poland-hungary-stand-united-except-on-russia-orban-szydlo/

Bayer, Lili, and Jacopo Barigazzi, "Central Europeans to Boycott Migration Summit They Weren't Invited to," *Politico*, June 21, 2018. As of July 18, 2018:
https://www.politico.eu/article/viktor-orban-hungary-poland-central-europeans-to-boycott-migration-summit-they-werent-invited-to/

Bergen, Peter, David Sterman, Alyssa Sims, and Albert Ford, *ISIS in the West: The Western Militant Flow to Syria and Iraq*, Washington, D.C.: New America, policy paper, March 2016. As of July 18, 2018:
https://www.newamerica.org/international-security/policy-papers/isis-in-the-west-march-2016/

Berman, Sheri, "Populism Is a Problem. Elitist Technocrats Aren't the Solution," *Foreign Policy*, December 20, 2017. As of July 18, 2018:
https://foreignpolicy.com/2017/12/20/populism-is-a-problem-elitist-technocrats-arent-the-solution/

Bershidsky, Leonid, "Europe's Anti-Kremlin Roll Call Was Weak," Bloomberg, March 27, 2018a. As of July 18, 2018:
https://www.bloomberg.com/view/articles/2018-03-27/russia-sanctions-europe-s-weak-response-to-the-skripal-poisoning

———, "The U.S. Should Move Troops from Germany to Poland," Bloomberg, May 30, 2018b. As of July 18, 2018:
https://www.bloomberg.com/view/articles/2018-05-30/why-the-u-s-should-move-its-troops-from-germany-to-poland

Bilyana, Lilly, and Jeremy Shapiro, "Sovereignty's Revenge: The Power of Populism in the European Union," Washington, D.C., Brookings Institution, April 30, 2015. As of July 18, 2018:
https://www.brookings.edu/blog/order-from-chaos/2015/04/30/sovereigntys-revenge-the-power-of-populism-in-the-european-union/

Black, James, Alexandra Hall, Kate Cox, Marta Kepe, and Erik Silfversten, *Defence and Security After Brexit: Understanding the Possible Implications of the UK's Decision to Leave the EU—Overview Report*, Santa Monica, Calif.: RAND Corporation, RR-1786/1-RC, 2017. As of July 17, 2018:
https://www.rand.org/pubs/research_reports/RR1786z1.html

Blanchard, Christopher M., *Saudi Arabia: Background and U.S. Relations*, Washington, D.C.: Congressional Research Service, CL33533, November 22, 2017. As of December 12, 2017:
https://fas.org/sgp/crs/mideast/RL33533.pdf

Blank, Jonah, Richard S. Girven, Arzan Tarapore, Julia A. Thompson, and Arthur Chan, *Vector Check: Prospects for U.S. and Pakistan Air Power Engagement*, Santa Monica, Calif.: RAND Corporation, RR-2107-AF, 2018. As of September 12, 2018:
https://www.rand.org/pubs/research_reports/RR2107.html

Blumenthal, Dan, "Economic Coercion as a Tool in China's Grand Strategy," statement before the Senate Committee on Foreign Relations, July 24, 2018. As of August 22, 2018:
https://www.foreign.senate.gov/imo/media/doc/072418_Blumenthal_Testimony.pdf

Brannon, Robert, *Russian Civil-Military Relations*, Farnham, UK: Ashgate, 2009.

Braw, Elisabeth, "Germany Is Quietly Building a European Army Under Its Command," *Foreign Affairs*, May 22, 2017a. As of July 18, 2018:
https://foreignpolicy.com/2017/05/22/germany-is-quietly-building-a-european-army-under-its-command/

———, "Europe's Readiness Problem," *Foreign Affairs*, November 30, 2017b. As of July 18, 2018:
https://www.foreignaffairs.com/articles/europe/2017-11-30/europes-readiness-problem

Bremmer, Ian, "The Hollow Alliance," *Time*, June 16, 2016. As of July 18, 2018:
http://time.com/4371195/nato-transatlantic-alliance-us-europe/

Brooks, Stephen G., and William C. Wohlforth, *World Out of Balance: International Relations and the Challenge of American Primacy*, Princeton, N.J.: Princeton University Press, 2008.

Brown, Nathan, "Egypt's Failed Transition," *Journal of Democracy*, Vol. 24, No. 4, October 2013, pp. 45–58.

Browne, Ryan, "Chinese Lasers Injure US Military Pilots in Africa, Pentagon Says," CNN, May 4, 2018. As of May 14, 2018:
https://www.cnn.com/2018/05/03/politics/chinese-lasers-us-military-pilots-africa/index.html

Brownlee, Jason, Tarek Masoud, and Andrew Reynolds, "Why the Modest Harvest?" *Journal of Democracy*, Vol. 24, No. 4, October 2013, pp. 29–44.

Bugge, Axel, "As Europe Left Struggles, Portugal's Alliance Wins Over Voters and Brussels," Reuters, March 31, 2017. As of July 18, 2018:
https://www.reuters.com/article/us-portugal-politics/as-europe-left-struggles-portugals-alliance-wins-over-voters-and-brussels-idUSKBN1721LF

Buras, Piotr, and Adam Balcer, "An Unpredictable Russia: The Impact on Poland," London, European Council on Foreign Relations, July 15, 2016. As of July 18, 2018: https://www.ecfr.eu/article/commentary_an_unpredictable_russia_the_impact_on_poland

Burr, William, "Sino-American Relations, 1969: The Sino-Soviet Border War and Steps Towards Rapprochement," *Cold War History*, Vol. 1, No. 3, 2001, pp. 73–112.

Cabinet Public Relations Office, *National Security Strategy*, Tokyo, December 17, 2013. As of November 16, 2017: http://japan.kantei.go.jp/96_abe/documents/2013/__icsFiles/afieldfile/2013/12/17/NSS.pdf

Caraballo, Mayvelin U., "China to Become PH's Principle Trade Partner," *Manila Times*, October 4, 2017. As of November 21, 2017: http://www.manilatimes.net/china-become-phs-principal-trade-partner/354474/

Carter, Erin Baggott, *Elite Welfare Shocks and Diversionary Foreign Policy: Evidence from China*, Los Angeles: University of Southern California, 2017. As of July 29, 2018: http://www.erinbcarter.org/documents/Diversion.pdf

Chaudon, Stephen, Helen V. Milner, and Dustin H. Tingley, "The Center Still Holds," *International Security*, Vol. 35, No. 1, Summer 2010, pp. 75–95.

Chazan, Guy, "CDU-CSU Spat Shakes Europe's Most Successful Electoral Alliance," *Financial Times*, June 18, 2018. As of July 18, 2018: https://www.ft.com/content/4397d4ba-72ed-11e8-b6ad-3823e4384287

Chernenko, Elena "«Za destabilizatsiei Ukrainy skryvaetsya popytka radikal'nogo oslableniya Rossii». Sekretar' Sovbeza RF Nikolai Patrushev o glavnykh ugrozakh dlya bezopasnosti Rossii" ["'The Destabilization of Ukraine Hides an Attempt to Radically Weaken Russia': Secretary of the Russian Security Council Nikolai Patrushev on the Main Threats to Russia's Security"], Kommersant.ru, June 22, 2015. As of February 3, 2018: https://www.kommersant.ru/doc/2752250

"China Focus: 'Be Ready to Win Wars,' China's Xi Orders Reshaped PLA," *Xinhua News*, August 1, 2017.

China, France, Germany, European Union, Iran, Russia, United Kingdom, and United States, *Joint Comprehensive Plan of Action*, Vienna, July 14, 2015. As of September 6, 2018: https://www.state.gov/documents/organization/245317.pdf

"China Is Reportedly Proposing a Permanent Military Base in the South Pacific," CNBC.com, April 9, 2018. As of May 14, 2018: https://www.cnbc.com/2018/04/09/china-is-reportedly-proposing-a-military-base-in-the-south-pacific.html

Christensen, Thomas J., "Windows and War: Trend Analysis and Beijing's Use of Force," in Alastair Iain Johnston and Robert S. Ross, eds., *New Directions in the Study of China's Foreign Policy*, Palo Alto, Calif.: Stanford University Press, 2006, pp. 50–85.

Chyong, Chi-Kong, Louisa Slavkova, and Vessela Tcherneva, "EU Alternatives to Russian Gas," London, European Council on Foreign Relations, April 9, 2015. As of July 18, 2018:
https://www.ecfr.eu/article/commentary_europes_alternatives_to_russian_gas311666

Clavel, Geoffroy, "France Supports Decision to Stay out of Iraq, but Doesn't Rule Out Future Conflicts," *Huffington Post*, March 19, 2013. As of July 18, 2018:
https://www.huffingtonpost.com/2013/03/19/iraq-war-france_n_2901205.html

Cohen, Ariel, and Robert E. Hamilton, *The Russian Military and the Georgia War: Lessons and Implications*, Carlisle, Pa.: Strategic Studies Institute, 2011.

Cohen, Raphael S., Nathan Chandler, Shira Efron, Bryan Frederick, Eugeniu Han, Kurt Klein, Forrest E. Morgan, Ashley L. Rhoades, Howard J. Shatz, and Yuliya Shokh, *The Future of Warfare in 2030: Project Overview and Conclusions*, Santa Monica, Calif.: RAND Corporation, RR-2849/1-AF, 2020. As of May 2020:
https://www.rand.org/pubs/research_reports/RR2849z1.html

Committee on Political Parties, *Toward a More Responsible Two-Party System*, Menesha, Wisc.: American Political Science Association, 1950.

Cornell, Svante E., and S. Frederick Starr, eds., *The Guns of August 2008*, Armonk, N.Y.: ME Sharpe, 2009.

Council of the European Union, "EU Fight Against Terrorism," webpage, March 20, 2018. As of July 12, 2018:
https://www.consilium.europa.eu/policies/fight-against-terrorism.aspx/?lang=en

Cozad, Mark R., and Nathan Beauchamp-Mustafaga, *People's Liberation Army Air Force Operations over Water: Maintaining Relevance in China's Changing Security Environment*, Santa Monica, Calif.: RAND Corporation, RR-2057-AF, 2017. As of December 4, 2018:
https://www.rand.org/pubs/research_reports/RR2057.html

Crone, Manni, Maja Felicia Falkentoft, and Teemu Tammikko, *European Citizens, Not Refugees, Behind Most Terrorist Attacks in Europe*, Copenhagen: Danish Institute for International Studies, June 21, 2017. As of July 18, 2018:
https://www.diis.dk/en/research/european-citizens-not-refugees-behind-most-terrorist-attacks-in-europe

Cronin, Patrick M., Richard Fontaine, Zachary M. Hosford, Oriana Skylar Mastro, Ely Ratner, and Alexander Sullivan, *The Emerging Asia Power Web: The Rise of Bilateral Intra-Asian Security Ties*, Washington, D.C.: Center for a New American Security, 2013. As of November 16, 2017:
https://www.files.ethz.ch/isn/165406/CNAS_AsiaPowerWeb.pdf

Dempsey, Judy, "Germany, Dump Nord Stream 2," *Judy Dempsey's Strategic Europe*, Carnegie Europe blog, January 25, 2016. As of July 18, 2018: https://carnegieeurope.eu/strategiceurope/62567

De Pinto, Jennifer, Fred Backus, Kabir Khanna, and Anthony Salvanto, "What Americans Think About U.S. Strike on Syria," CBS News, April 10, 2017. As of November 8, 2017:
https://www.cbsnews.com/news/cbs-news-poll-shows-divergence-in-americans-opinion-of-us-strike-vs-syria/

Dobbins, James, David C. Gompert, David A. Shlapak, and Andrew Scobell, *Conflict with China: Prospects, Consequences, and Strategies for Deterrence*, Santa Monica, Calif.: RAND Arroyo Center, OP-344-A, 2011. As of December 4, 2018: https://www.rand.org/pubs/occasional_papers/OP344.html

Dobbins, James, Andrew Scobell, Edmund J. Burke, David C. Gompert, Derek Grossman, Eric Heginbotham, and Howard J. Shatz, *Conflict with China Revisited: Prospects, Consequences, and Strategies for Deterrence*, Santa Monica, Calif.: RAND Corporation, PE-248-A, 2017. As of December 4, 2018: https://www.rand.org/pubs/perspectives/PE248.html

DPA and Reuters, "NATO Says More Members Plan to Reach Spending Goal by 2024," RadioFreeEurope, February 14, 2018. As of July 18, 2018: https://www.rferl.org/a/fifteen-of-29-nato-members-meet-defense-spending-goal-2-percent-gdp-by-2024-stoltenberg-says-mattis-pressure-brussels-meeting/29038749.html

Drake, Bruce, and Carroll Doherty, "Key Findings on How Americans View the U.S. Role in the World," Washington, D.C., Pew Research Center, May 5, 2016. As of November 9, 2017:
http://www.pewresearch.org/fact-tank/2016/05/05/key-findings-on-how-americans-view-the-u-s-role-in-the-world/

Dunlop, John, *The Moscow Bombings of September 1999: Examinations of Russian Terrorist Attacks at the Onset of Vladimir Putin's Rule*, Vol. 110, New York: Columbia University Press, 2014.

Dutton, Peter, "Three Disputes and Three Objectives—China and the South China Sea," *Naval War College Review*, Vol. 64, No. 4, 2011, pp. 42–67.

Economy, Elizabeth C., "China's New Revolution: The Reign of Xi Jinping," *Foreign Affairs*, Vol. 97, No. 3, May–June 2018, pp. 60–74.

Efron, Shira, Kurt Klein, and Raphael S. Cohen, *Environment, Geography, and the Future of Warfare: The Changing Global Environment and Its Implications for the U.S. Air Force*, Santa Monica, Calif.: RAND Corporation, RR-2849/5-AF, 2020. As of May 2020:
https://www.rand.org/pubs/research_reports/RR2849z5.html

Egorov, Ivan, "Patrushev: Popytki ustroit' "tsvetnye revolyutsii" v Rossii besperspektivny" ["Patrushev: Attempts to Incite 'Color Revolutions' in Russia Are Useless"], *Rossiskaya Gazeta*, May 18, 2017. As of January 26, 2018: https://rg.ru/2017/05/18/patrushev-popytki-ustroit-cvetnye-revoliucii-v-rossii-besperspektivny.html

Ellyatt, Holly, "China's Slowing Demand for Oil Is a Serious Concern for the Middle East," CNBC, September 3, 2018. As of October 24, 2018: https://www.cnbc.com/2018/09/03/china-demand-for-oil-is-a-serious-concern-for-the-middle-east.html

Embassy of the People's Republic of China in the United States of America, "国防部：大陆对台湾军事部署是否调整将视情况而定" ["Ministry of Defense: Adjustments to Mainland Military Disposition Toward Taiwan Will Depend on the Situation"], Washington, D.C., 2008. As of March 27, 2018: http://www.china-embassy.org/chn/zt/twwt/t709316.htm

Erlanger, Steven, "Migration to Europe Is Slowing, but the Political Issue Is as Toxic as Ever," *New York Times*, June 22, 2018. As of July 18, 2018: https://www.nytimes.com/2018/06/22/world/europe/migration-europe-merkel-seehofer-germany.html

"EU to Sue Poland, Hungary, and Czechs for Refusing Refugee Quotas," BBC, December 7, 2017. As of July 18, 2018: https://www.bbc.com/news/world-europe-42270239

European Parliament, "Survey: People Reveal Their Priorities for the EU," news blog, January 7, 2016. As of July 18, 2018: http://www.europarl.europa.eu/news/en/headlines/eu-affairs/20160630STO34203/survey-people-reveal-their-priorities-for-the-eu

———, "EU Migrant Crisis: Facts and Figures," news blog, June 30, 2017. As of July 18, 2018: http://www.europarl.europa.eu/news/en/headlines/society/20170629STO78630/eu-migrant-crisis-facts-and-figures

European Union Agency for Law Enforcement Cooperation, "European Counter Terrorism Centre—ECTC," webpage, undated. As of July 18, 2018: https://www.europol.europa.eu/about-europol/european-counter-terrorism-centre-ectc

———, *European Union Serious and Organised Crime Assessment 2017*, The Hague, 2017. As of July 18, 2018: https://www.europol.europa.eu/activities-services/main-reports/european-union-serious-and-organised-crime-threat-assessment-2017

Eurostat, "Migration and Migrant Population Statistics," webpage, undated. As of July 18, 2018: http://ec.europa.eu/eurostat/statistics-explained/index.php/Migration_and_migrant_population_statistics

Executive Office of the President, *National Security Strategy*, Washington, D.C., 2017.

Eyal, Jonathan, "The Other Europe? How Central Europe Views the Continent's Security Concerns and Aspirations," *RUSI Newsbrief*, Vol. 38, No. 5, June 25, 2018. As of July 18, 2018:
https://rusi.org/publication/newsbrief/other-europe-how-central-europe-views-continents-security-concerns-and

Fei, John, "China's Overseas Military Base in Djibouti: Features, Motivations, and Policy Implications," *China Brief*, Vol. 17, No. 17, December 22, 2017.

Feleke, Bethlehem, "China Tests Bombers on South China Sea Island," CNN, May 21, 2018. As of May 22, 2018:
https://www.cnn.com/2018/05/20/asia/south-china-sea-bombers-islands-intl/index.html

Fiorina, Morris P., and Samuel J. Abrams, "Political Polarization in the American Public," *Annual Review of Political Science*, Vol. 11, 2008, pp. 563–588.

"Flirting with Polexit? Poland's President Wants a Referendum on the EU: Most Poles Are Keen to Stay," *The Economist*, June 20, 2018. As of July 18, 2018:
https://www.economist.com/news/europe/21744799-most-poles-are-keen-stay-polands-president-wants-referendum-eu

Flood, Rebecca, "Shock Figures: Seven Out of 10 Migrants Crossing to Europe Are Not Refugees, UN Reveals," *Daily Express*, July 4, 2017. As of July 18, 2018:
https://www.express.co.uk/news/world/824794/migrant-crisis-refugee-Italy-Libya-UN-figures-Mediterranean-boat-crossing

"France's Response to Terrorism: Loss of Faith," *The Economist*, July 30, 2016. As of July 18, 2018:
https://www.economist.com/europe/2016/07/30/loss-of-faith

Fravel, M. Taylor, "Power Shifts and Escalation: Explaining China's Use of Force in Territorial Disputes," *International Security*, Vol. 32, No. 3, 2008, pp. 44–83.

Frederick, Bryan, and Nathan Chandler, *Restraint and the Future of Warfare: The Changing Global Environment and Its Implications for the U.S. Air Force*, Santa Monica, Calif.: RAND Corporation, RR-2849/6-AF, 2020. As of May 2020:
https://www.rand.org/pubs/research_reports/RR2849z6.html

Friedberg, Aaron L., "Ripe for Rivalry: Prospects for Peace in a Multipolar Asia," *International Security*, Vol. 18, No. 3, Winter 1993/1994, pp. 5–33.

Fuchs, Richard, "Germany's Russian Energy Dilemma," *Deutsche Welle*, March 29, 2014. As of July 18, 2018:
https://www.dw.com/en/germanys-russian-energy-dilemma/a-17529685

Gady, F., "Iran Deploys New Russian Air Defense System Around Nuclear Site," *The Diplomat*, August 31, 2016.

Galeotti, Mark, *Russia's Wars in Chechnya 1994–2009*, Oxford, UK: Osprey, 2014.

———, *Controlling Chaos: How Russia Manages Its Political War in Europe*, London: European Council on Foreign Relations, September 1, 2017. As of July 18, 2018:
https://www.ecfr.eu/publications/summary/controlling_chaos_how_russia_manages_its_political_war_in_europe

Gallup, "Confidence in Institutions," webpage, undated-a. As of November 8, 2017:
http://news.gallup.com/poll/1597/Confidence-Institutions.aspx

———, "U.S. Position in the World," webpage, undated-b. As of November 9, 2017:
http://news.gallup.com/poll/116350/position-world.aspx

Galston, William A., "The Rise of European Populism and the Collapse of the Center-Left," Washington, D.C., Brookings Institution, news blog, March 8, 2018. As of July 18, 2018:
https://www.brookings.edu/blog/order-from-chaos/2018/03/08/the-rise-of-european-populism-and-the-collapse-of-the-center-left/

Ganguly, Sumit, "India After Nonalignment: Why Modi Skipped the Summit," *Foreign Affairs*, September 19, 2016. As of November 22, 2017:
https://www.foreignaffairs.com/print/1118315

Gao, Charlie, "Poland Wants Lots of U.S. Military Gear; The Reason: Russia," *National Interest*, June 30, 2018. As of July 18, 2018:
https://nationalinterest.org/blog/buzz/poland-wants-lots-us-military-gear-reason-russia-24702

Garver, John W., *Foreign Relations of the People's Republic of China*, Vol. 9, Englewood Cliffs, N.J.: Prentice Hall, 1993.

Gause, F. Gregory, III, "The Future of U.S. Saudi Relations: The Kingdom and the Power," *Foreign Affairs*, June 13, 2016. As of December 6, 2017:
https://www.foreignaffairs.com/print/1117547

Gerasimov, Valerii, "Tsennost' nauki v predvidenii" ["The Value of Science Is in Foresight"], *Voenno-Promyshlennyi Kurer [Military Industrial Courier]*, February 27, 2013. As of January 3, 2018:
https://vpk.name/news/85159_cennost_nauki_v_predvidenii.html

"Germans Least Supportive of Defending Allies Against Russia," webpage, Pew Research Center, May 22, 2017. As of July 18, 2018:
http://www.pewglobal.org/2017/05/23/natos-image-improves-on-both-sides-of-atlantic/pg_2017-05-23-nato-00-03/

Gillingham, John, and Marian L. Tupy, "The EU Will Likely Implode," *The National Interest*, February 25, 2016. As of July 18, 2018:
https://nationalinterest.org/feature/the-eu-will-likely-implode-15314

Glaser, Bonnie S., and Lisa Collins, "China's Rapprochement with South Korea: Who Won the THAAD Dispute?" *Foreign Affairs*, November 7, 2017. As of November 28, 2017:
https://www.foreignaffairs.com/print/1121331

"Glava "Rostekha" soobshchil o roste prodazh: "Chem bol'she konfliktov, tem bol'she u nas pokupayut vooruzheniya" ["The Head of Rostech on Growing Arms Sales: "The More Conflicts There Are, the More They Buy Our Weapons"], News.ru, February 23, 2015. As of February 4, 2018:
http://www.newsru.com/russia/23feb2015/chemezov.html

Gompert, David C., Astrid Stuth Cevallos, and Cristina L. Garafola, *War with China: Thinking Through the Unthinkable*, Santa Monica, Calif.: RAND Corporation, RR-1140-A, 2016. As of December 4, 2018:
https://www.rand.org/pubs/research_reports/RR1140.html

Goodwin, Matthew, "Ukip Is Back Thanks to the Chequers Backlash," *Spectator*, July 28, 2018. As of September 12, 2018:
https://www.spectator.co.uk/2018/07/ukip-is-back-thanks-to-the-chequers-backlash/

Gordon, Michael, and Jeremy Page, "China Installed Military Jamming Equipment on Spratly Islands, U.S. Says," *Wall Street Journal*, April 9, 2018. As of May 14, 2018:
https://www.wsj.com/articles/china-installed-military-jamming-equipment-on-spratly-islands-u-s-says-1523266320

Gressel, Gustav, "Austria: Russia's Trojan Horse?" London, European Council on Foreign Relations, December 21, 2017. As of July 18, 2018:
https://www.ecfr.eu/article/commentary_austria_russias_trojan_horse

Gribble, Rachael, Simon Wessley, Susan Klein, David A. Alexander, Christopher Dandeker, and Nicola T. Fear, "British Public Opinion After a Decade of War: Attitudes to Iraq and Afghanistan," *Politics: 2014*, Vol. 35, No. 2, 2015. As of July 18, 2018:
http://journals.sagepub.com/doi/abs/10.1111/1467-9256.12073?journalCode=pola

Grigas, Agnia, *Beyond Crimea: The New Russian Empire*, New Haven, Conn.: Yale University Press, 2016.

Gurzu, Anca, "Germany's Double Gas Game with Russia," *Politico*, March 28, 2018. As of July 18, 2018:
https://www.politico.eu/article/germany-russia-gas-nord-stream-2-foreign-policy/

Harding, Robert, "Japan Scrambles Record Number of Jets as Tensions Rise with China," *Financial Times*, April 13, 2017. As of April 2, 2018:
https://www.ft.com/content/f7fb3d7a-2014-11e7-a454-ab04428977f9

Harel, Amos, "Israel Signals Lull in Syria Strikes Is Over, Resuming Military Action Against Iran," *Ha'aretz*, September 5, 2018. As of September 6, 2018: https://www.haaretz.com/middle-east-news/syria/.premium-israel-signals-lull-in-syria-strikes-is-over-resuming-military-action-1.6445288

Hauer, Neil, "Russia's Mercenary Debacle in Syria: Is the Kremlin Losing Control?" *Foreign Affairs*, February 26, 2018. As of March 13, 2018: https://www.foreignaffairs.com/articles/syria/2018-02-26/russias-mercenary-debacle-syria

Herszenhorn, David, "Warsaw to Trump: Let's Make a Military Deal (Without NATO)," *Politico*, May 30, 2018. As of July 18, 2018: https://www.politico.eu/article/warsaw-poland-andrzej-duda-to-donald-trump-lets-make-a-military-deal-without-nato/

Herszenhorn, David, and Maia de la Baume, "Juncker and Selmayr Fight Timmermans on Behalf of Poland," *Politico*, June 8, 2018. As of July 18, 2018: https://www.politico.eu/article/jean-claude-juncker-martin-selmayr-fight-frans-timmermans-on-behalf-of-poland/

Heydarian, Richard Javad, "Duterte's Dance with China: Why the Philippines Won't Abandon Washington," *Foreign Affairs*, April 26, 2016. As of July 2, 2018: https://www.foreignaffairs.com/articles/philippines/2017-04-26/dutertes-dance-china

Hikotani, Takako, "Trump's Gift to Japan," *Foreign Affairs*, Vol. 96, No. 5, September/October 2017. As of November 15, 2017: https://www.foreignaffairs.com/articles/asia/2017-08-15/trumps-gift-japan

Hill, Fiona, "This Is What Putin Really Wants," Washington, D.C., Brookings Institution, February 24, 2015. As of July 18, 2018: https://www.brookings.edu/opinions/this-is-what-putin-really-wants/

Hong Hiep, Le, "Vietnam's Strategic Trajectory: From Internal Development to External Engagement," *Strategic Insights*, No. 59, June 2012. As of November 15, 2017: https://www.files.ethz.ch/isn/161731/SI59_Vietnam.pdf

Hsueh, Roselyn, "Taiwan's Treaty Trouble: The Backlash Against Taipei's China Deal," *Foreign Affairs*, June 3, 2014. As of November 15, 2017: https://www.foreignaffairs.com/articles/china/2014-06-03/taiwans-treaty-trouble

Humud, Carla E., Christopher M. Blanchard, and Mary Beth D. Nikitin, *Armed Conflict in Syria: Overview and U.S. Response*, Washington, D.C.: Congressional Research Service, RL33487, October 13, 2017. As of December 11, 2017: https://fas.org/sgp/crs/mideast/RL33487.pdf

"In Austria, Russia Hopes to Exploit Europe's Divisions," Stratfor, June 23, 2014. As of July 18, 2018: https://worldview.stratfor.com/article/austria-russia-hopes-exploit-europes-divisions

International Institute for Strategic Studies, *The Military Balance 2017*, London: February 2017.

International Monetary Fund, European Department, *Russian Federation: 2018 Article IV Consultation—Press Release; Staff Report*, Paris, September 12, 2018. As of October 24, 2018:
https://www.imf.org/en/Publications/CR/Issues/2018/09/12/Russian-Federation-2018-Article-IV-Consultation-Press-Release-Staff-Report-46226

Jane's IHS Markit, "Terror Risks in Europe to Increase in 2018 as Islamic State's Foreign Fighters Return," press release, February 13, 2018. As of July 18, 2018:
http://www.janes.com/article/77853/terror-risks-in-europe-to-increase-in-2018-as-islamic-state-s-foreign-fighters-return-jane-s-by-ihs-markit-says

Japan-US Alliance Study Group, *The Trump Administration and Japan: Challenges and Visions for Japan's Foreign and Security Policy in the New Era*, Tokyo: Institute for International Policy Studies, 2017. As of November 16, 2017:
http://www.iips.org/en/research/usjr2017en.pdf

Jeong, Gyung-Ho, and Paul J. Quirk, "Division at the Water's Edge: The Polarization of Foreign Policy," *American Politics Research*, July 2017, pp. 1–30.

Jian, Chen, "China's Involvement in the Vietnam War, 1964–69," China Quarterly, Vol. 142, 1995a, pp. 356–387.

———, *China's Road to the Korean War: The Making of the Sino-American Confrontation*, New York: Columbia University Press, 1995b.

Jinping, Xi, "Secure a Decisive Victory in Building a Moderately Prosperous Society in All Respects and Strive for the Great Success of Socialism with Chinese Characteristics for a New Era," speech delivered at the 19th National Congress of the Communist Party of China, October 18, 2017. As of May 14, 2018:
http://www.xinhuanet.com/english/download/Xi_Jinping%27s_report_at_19th_CPC_National_Congress.pdf

Johnston, Alastair Iain, *Cultural Realism: Strategic Culture and Grand Strategy in Chinese History*, Princeton, N.J.: Princeton University Press, 1998.

Jones, Seth G., "Will al Qaeda Make a Comeback? The Factors That Will Determine Its Success," *Foreign Affairs*, August 7, 2017. As December 8, 2017:
https://www.foreignaffairs.com/print/1120608

Juergensmeyer, Mark, *Terror in the Mind of God: The Global Rise of Religious Violence*, 4th ed., Oakland, Calif.: University of California Press, 2017.

Kang, David C., "Getting Asia Wrong: The Need for New Analytical Frameworks," *International Security*, Vol. 27, No. 4, Spring 2003, pp. 57–85.

Katzman, Kenneth, *Iran's Foreign and Defense Policies*, Washington, D.C.: Congressional Research Service, R44017, November 7, 2017. As of December 12, 2017:
https://fas.org/sgp/crs/mideast/R44017.pdf

Katzman, Kenneth, and Carla E. Humud, *Iraq: Politics and Governance*, Washington, D.C., Congressional Research Service, RS21960, March 9, 2016. As of December 11, 2017:
https://fas.org/sgp/crs/mideast/RS21968.pdf

Katzman, Kenneth, and Clayton Thomas, *Afghanistan: Post-Taliban Governance, Security and U.S. Policy*, Washington, D.C.: Congressional Research Service, RL30588, November 7, 2017. As of December 12, 2017:
https://fas.org/sgp/crs/row/RL30588.pdf

Kershner, Isabel, and Thomas Erdbrink, "As Deadline on Nuclear Deal Nears, Israel and Iran Issue Warnings," *New York Times*, May 6, 2018. As of September 6, 2018:
https://www.nytimes.com/2018/05/06/world/middleeast/israel-iran-nuclear-deal.html

Kirkpatrick, David D., "Saudi Arabia Charges Iran with 'Act of War,' Raising Threat of Military Clash," *New York Times*, November 6, 2017. As of December 15, 2017:
https://www.nytimes.com/2017/11/06/world/middleeast/yemen-saudi-iran-missile.html

Kissinger, Henry, and Nicholas Hormann, *On China*, New York: Penguin Press, 2011.

Korteweg, Rem, "The EU and Transatlantic Relations," Centre for European Reform, February 20, 2013.

Krauthammer, Charles, "The Unipolar Moment," *Foreign Affairs*, Vol. 70, No. 1, 1990/1991, pp. 23–33.

Krechetnikov, A., "Brosok na Prishtinu: na grani voiny" ["March to Pristina: At the Brink of War"], Russkaya Sluzhba BBC, June 11, 2014. As of January 18, 2018:
http://www.bbc.com/russian/international/2014/06/140610_pristina_march_anniversary

Kronstad, K. Alan, and Shayerah Ilias Akhtar, *India-U.S. Relations: Issues for Congress*, Washington, D.C.: Congressional Research Service, R44876, June 19, 2017. As of November 22, 2017:
https://fas.org/sgp/crs/row/R44876.pdf

Kupchan, Charles A., and Peter L. Trubowitz, "Dead Center and the Demise of Liberal Internationalism," *International Security*, Vol. 32, No. 2, Fall 2007, pp. 7–44.

———, "The Illusion of Liberal Internationalism's Revival," *International Security*, Vol. 35, No. 1, Summer 2010, pp. 95–109.

Lengxi, Wu, "Inside Story of the Decision Making During the Shelling of Jinmen," *Zhuanji Wenxue [Biographical Literature]*, No. 1, 1994, pp. 5–11.

Liao, Jessica C., "The Filipino Fox: There's a Method to Duterte's Madness," *Foreign Affairs*, January 18, 2017. As of November 20, 2017: https://www.foreignaffairs.com/print/1119217

Lynch, Daniel, "Why Ma Won the Elections and What's Next for Taiwan and China," *Foreign Affairs*, January 15, 2012. As of November 15, 2017: https://www.foreignaffairs.com/articles/china/2012-01-15/why-ma-won-elections-and-whats-next-taiwan-and-china

Major, Claudia, and Christian Molling, "The Framework Nations Concept," *SWP Comments*, No. 52, December 2014. As of July 18, 2018: https://www.swp-berlin.org/fileadmin/contents/products/comments/2014C52_mjr_mlg.pdf

Mansfield, Edward D., and Jack Snyder, *Electing to Fight: Why Emerging Democracies Go to War*, Cambridge, Mass.: MIT Press, 2005.

Manyin, Mark E., Emma Chanlett-Avery, Mary Beth D. Nikitin, Brock R. Williams, and Jonathan R. Corrado, *U.S.-South Korea Relations*, Washington, D.C.: Congressional Research Service, R41481, May 23, 2017. As of November 29, 2017: https://fas.org/sgp/crs/row/R41481.pdf

March, Luke, "2016: The Ebbing of Europe's Radical Left Tide?" *European Futures*, blog post, Edinburgh Europa Institute, November 7, 2016. As of July 18, 2018: http://www.europeanfutures.ed.ac.uk/article-4395

Marston, Hunter, "Why Tensions Are Rising Between Vietnam and China," *Foreign Affairs*, August 15, 2017. As of November 15, 2017: https://www.foreignaffairs.com/articles/asia/2017-08-15/why-tensions-are-rising-between-vietnam-and-china

Martewicz, Maciej, "Poland Waves Goodbye to Russian Gas After 74 Years," Bloomberg, February 8, 2018. As of July 18, 2018: https://www.bloomberg.com/news/articles/2018-02-08/poland-bets-on-lng-norwegian-gas-as-divorce-with-russia-looms

Mason, Shane, "India's Achilles' Heel: New Delhi Lags on Defense," *Foreign Affairs*, March 22, 2016. As of November 22, 2017: https://www.foreignaffairs.com/print/1117038

Mazarr, Michael J., Jonathan Blake, Abigail Casey, Tim McDonald, Stephanie Pezard, and Michael Spirtas, *Understanding the Emerging Era of International Competition: Theoretical and Historical Perspectives*, Santa Monica, Calif.: RAND Corporation, RR-2726-AF, 2018.

Mazza, Michael, "Chinese Check: Forging New Identities in Hong Kong and Taiwan," *The American*, October 14, 2014. As November 15, 2017: https://www.aei.org/publication/chinese-check-forging-new-identities-hong-kong-taiwan-2/print/

Mazzetti, Mark, and Matt Apuzzo, "U.S. Relies Heavily on Saudi Money to Support Syrian Rebels," *New York Times*, January 23, 2016. December 15, 2017: https://www.nytimes.com/2016/01/24/world/middleeast/us-relies-heavily-on-saudi-money-to-support-syrian-rebels.html

McClosky, Herbert, "Consensus and Ideology in American Politics," *American Political Science Review*, Vol. 58, No. 2, June 1964, pp. 361–382.

Miller, Elissa, and Kevin Truitte, "Filling the Vacuum in Libya," *Foreign Affairs*, July 18, 2017. As of December 8, 2017: https://www.foreignaffairs.com/print/1120484

Miller, J. Berkshire, "Japan Warms to China," *Foreign Affairs*, July 17, 2017. As of November 15, 2017: https://www.foreignaffairs.com/articles/asia/2017-07-17/japan-warms-china

Ministry of Defence, *Strategic Trends Programme: Global Strategic Trends—Out to 2045*, 5th ed., London, April 30, 2014. As of December 18, 2018: https://espas.secure.europarl.europa.eu/orbis/sites/default/files/generated/document/en/MinofDef_Global%20Strategic%20Trends%20-%202045.pdf

Ministry of Defense of the Russian Federation, "Ministr oborony Rossii vystupil s lektsiei na otkrytii II Vserossiiskogo molodezhnogo foruma v MGIMO" ["Russian Defense Minister Gave a Lecture at the Opening of the II All-Russian Youth Forum at MGIMO"], February 21, 2017a. As of January 4, 2018: https://function.mil.ru/news_page/person/more.htm?id=12112529@egNews

———, Twitter, 3 a.m., December 26, 2017b. As of March 20, 2018: https://twitter.com/mod_russia/status/945610297309528069

Ministry of Foreign Affairs of the Russian Federation, Military Doctrine of the Russian Federation, No. Pr.-2976, December 25, 2014. As of January 8, 2019: https://rusemb.org.uk/press/2029

———, *Kontseptsiya vneshnei politiki Rossiiskoi Federatsii [Foreign Policy Concept of the Russian Federation]*, approved by President of the Russian Federation Vladimir Putin on November 30, 2016, December 1, 2016.

Ministry of National Defense of the People's Republic of China, "胜战之问" ["The Issue of Successful War"], August 2, 2017. As of April 2, 2018 (in Chinese): http://www.mod.gov.cn/jmsd/2017-08/02/content_4787667.htm

Mohseni, Payam, and Hussein Kalout, "Iran's Axis of Resistance Rises: How It's Forging a New Middle East," *Foreign Affairs*, October 23, 2017. As of December 7, 2017: https://www.foreignaffairs.com/print/1119254

Monteiro, Nuno P., "Unrest Assured: Why Unipolarity Is Not Peaceful," *International Security*, Vol. 36, No. 3, Winter 2011/2012, pp. 9–40.

Morgan, Forrest E., and Raphael S. Cohen, *Military Trends and the Future of Warfare: The Changing Global Environment and Its Implications for the U.S. Air Force*, Santa Monica, Calif.: RAND Corporation, RR-2849/3-AF, 2020. As of May 2020:
https://www.rand.org/pubs/research_reports/RR2849z3.html

Morris, Ian, "Why Europe's Great Experiment Is Failing," Stratfor, January 27, 2016. As of July 18, 2018:
https://worldview.stratfor.com/article/why-europes-great-experiment-failing

Mount, Adam, "How to Put the U.S.–South Korean Alliance Back on Track and What to Expect from the Trump-Moon Summit," *Foreign Affairs*, June 28, 2017. As of November 28, 2017:
https://www.foreignaffairs.com/print/1120393

Mueller, John, "War Has Almost Ceased to Exist: An Assessment," *Political Science Quarterly*, Vol. 124, No. 2, 2009, pp. 297–321.

Myre, Greg, "Taking U.S. Politics Beyond 'The Water's Edge,'" NPR, March 10, 2015. As of November 6, 2017:
http://www.npr.org/sections/parallels/2015/03/10/392095906/taking-u-s-politics-beyond-the-waters-edge

Nasseri, Ladane, Golnar Motevalli, and Arsalan Shahla, "After Sanctions, Iran's Economy Is Nearing a Crisis," Bloomberg, August 9, 2018. As of September 6, 2018:
https://www.bloomberg.com/news/articles/2018-08-09/as-sanctions-hit-iran-s-on-the-verge-of-economic-breakdown

NATO—*See* North Atlantic Treaty Organization.

Neuhauser, Alan, "EIA: U.S. Net Oil Imports to Drop to Lowest Levels in 60 Years," *US News*, July 18, 2018. As of October 25, 2018:
https://www.usnews.com/news/national-news/articles/2018-07-10/eia-us-net-oil-imports-to-drop-to-lowest-levels-in-60-years

Nichol, Jim, *Russia-Georgia Conflict in South Ossetia: Context and Implications for U.S. Interests*, Washington, D.C.: Congressional Research Service, RL34618, August 29, 2008.

Noack, Rick, "Afraid of a Major Conflict? The German Military Is Currently Unavailable," *Washington Post*, January 24, 2018. As of July 18, 2018:
https://www.washingtonpost.com/news/worldviews/wp/2018/01/24/afraid-of-a-major-conflict-the-german-military-is-currently-unavailable/?utm_term=.5374ca0fe0a5

North Atlantic Treaty Organization, Statement by NATO Secretary General Dr. Javier Solana on Suspension of Air Operations, press release 093, June 10, 1999. As of December 5, 2018:
https://www.nato.int/kosovo/press/p990610a.htm

———, “Defence Expenditure of NATO Countries (2010–2017),” press release 111, June 29, 2017. As of July 18, 2018:
https://www.nato.int/cps/en/natohq/news_145409.htm

Office of the Director of National Intelligence, “Paradox of Progress, Near Future: Tensions Are Rising, Growing Terrorism Threat,” *Global Trends Main Report*, undated. As of July 18, 2018:
https://www.dni.gov/index.php/global-trends/near-future

———, “Assessing Russian Activities and Intentions in Recent US Elections,” Washington, D.C., Intelligence Community Assessment, January 6, 2017. As of March 21, 2018:
https://www.dni.gov/files/documents/ICA_2017_01.pdf

Office of the United Nations High Commissioner for Refugees, *Mixed Migration Trends in Libya: Changing Dynamics and Protection Challenges*, Geneva: July 2017. As of July 18, 2018:
http://www.unhcr.org/en-us/publications/operations/595a02b44/mixed-migration-trends-libya-changing-dynamics-protection-challenges.html

O’Rourke, Ronald, *Maritime Territorial and Exclusive Economic Zone (EEZ) Disputes Involving China: Issues for Congress*, Washington, D.C.: Congressional Research Service, R42784, September 15, 2017. As of November 20, 2017:
http://www.dtic.mil/dtic/tr/fulltext/u2/a624220.pdf

———, *China’s Actions in South and East China Seas: Implications for U.S. Interests—Background and Issues for Congress*, Washington, D.C.: Congressional Research Service, R42784, August 1, 2018. As of August 8, 2018:
https://fas.org/sgp/crs/row/R42784.pdf

Palacios, Maria Carmen Martin, “What Would Happen to Security in Europe If the European Union Broke Up?” *Sigma Iota Rho Journal of International Relations*, September 27, 2017. As of July 18, 2018:
http://www.sirjournal.org/research/2017/9/27/what-would-happen-to-security-in-europe-if-the-european-union-broke-up

Pandit, Rajat, “India to Go Ahead with S-400 Missile Deal with Russia Despite US Pressure,” *Times of India*, July 13, 2018. As of September 12, 2018:
http://timesofindia.indiatimes.com/articleshow/64978620.cms?utm_source=contentofinterest&utm_medium=text&utm_campaign=cppst

Paul, Christopher, and Miriam Matthews, *The Russian “Firehose of Falsehood” Propaganda Model: Why It Might Work and Options to Counter It*, Santa Monica, Calif.: RAND Corporation, PE-198-OSD, 2016.

Peet, John, “Creaking at 60: The Future of the European Union,” *The Economist*, March 25, 2017. As of July 18, 2018:
https://www.economist.com/special-report/2017/03/25/the-future-of-the-european-union

"PetroVietnam Targets 13.28 Million Tonnes of Crude Oil in 2017," *Saigon Online*, July 14, 2017. As of November 20, 2017: http://sggpnews.org.vn/business/petrovietnam-targets-1328-million-tonnes-of-crude-oil-in-2017-67840.html

Pew Research Center, "Global Indicators Database: Opinion of the United States—Do You Have a Favorable or Unfavorable View of the U.S.?" webpage, Spring 2017. As of January 9, 2018: http://www.pewglobal.org/database/indicator/1/

Piazza, James A., "Draining the Swamp: Democracy Promotion, State Failure, and Terrorism in 19 Middle Eastern Countries," *Studies in Conflict & Terrorism*, Vol. 30, No. 6, 2007, pp. 521–539.

Pinker, Steven, *The Better Angels of Our Nature: Why Violence Has Declined*, New York: Penguin Books, 2012.

"Poland About to Increase Its Defence Expenditure up to the Level of 2.5% of GDP: A New Bill Introduced," Defence24.com, April 24, 2017. As of July 18, 2018: https://www.defence24.com/poland-about-to-increase-its-defence-expenditure-up-to-the-level-of-25-of-gdp-a-new-bill-introduced

"Poland Will Increase the Size of Its Military by over 50%," *Global Security Review*, November 16, 2017. As of July 18, 2018: https://globalsecurityreview.com/poland-will-increase-size-military-50/

Politi, James, "Five Star and League Take Power in Italy," *Financial Times*, June 1, 2018. As of July 18, 2018: https://www.ft.com/content/2b7bd3d0-65ab-11e8-90c2-9563a0613e56

"Political Polarization in the American Public," webpage, Pew Research Center, June 12, 2014. As of November 8, 2017: http://www.people-press.org/2014/06/12/political-polarization-in-the-american-public/

Politkovskaya, Anna, *A Small Corner of Hell: Dispatches from Chechnya*, Chicago: University of Chicago Press, 2007.

Popov, I., and M. Khamzatov, *Voina budushchego. Kontseptual'nye osnovy i prakticheskie vyvody [The War of the Future: Conceptual Foundations and Practical Considerations]*, Moscow: Kuchkovo Pole, 2016.

"Press-konferentsiya Vladimira Putina dlya rossiiskikh i inostrannykh zhurnalistov" ["Vladimir Putin's Press Conference for Russian and Foreign Journalists"], Kremlin.ru, December 23, 2004. As of February 1, 2018: http://kremlin.ru/events/president/transcripts/22757

Prins, Gwythian, "The EU Is at Clear Risk of Collapse—And the 'Remainiacs' Just Don't See It," *Briefings for Brexit*, April 2018. As of July 18, 2018: https://briefingsforbrexit.com/the-eu-is-at-clear-risk-of-collapse-and-the-remainiacs-just-dont-see-it/

Public Law 107-40, Authorization for Use of Military Force Against Terrorists, September 18, 2001. As of November 7, 2017:
https://www.gpo.gov/fdsys/pkg/PLAW-107publ40/pdf/PLAW-107publ40.pdf

"Public Sees U.S. Power Declining as Support for Global Engagement Slips," webpage, Pew Research Center, December 3, 2013. As of November 9, 2017:
http://www.people-press.org/2013/12/03/
public-sees-u-s-power-declining-as-support-for-global-engagement-slips/

"Putin rasskazal, kak SShA podderzhivali terroristov v Chechne" ["Putin Told How U.S. Were Supporting Chechen Terrorists"], *Ria Novosti*, June 13, 2017. As of February 4, 2018:
https://ria.ru/politics/20170613/1496357892.html?inj=1

"Putin ratifitsiroval soglashenie RF i Abkhazii ob ob"edinennoi gruppirovke voisk" ["Putin Ratified the Agreement Between RF and Abkhazia on 'Joint Force'"], Interfax.ru, November 22, 2016. As of February 9, 2018:
http://www.interfax.ru/russia/538086

Putin, Vladimir, "Vystuplenie na zasedanii kluba 'Valdai'" ["Speech at the Valdai Club Meeting"], September 19, 2013. As of March 15, 2018:
http://kremlin.ru/events/president/news/19243

———, "Poslanie Prezidenta Federal'nomu Sobraniyu" ["President's Message to the Federal Assembly"], Kremlin.ru, December 4, 2014.

———, "Poslanie Prezidenta Federal'nomu Sobraniyu" ["President's Message to the Federal Assembly"], Kremlin.ru, March 1, 2018.

Radin, Andrew, Lynn E. Davis, Edward Geist, Eugeniu Han, Dara Massicot, Matthew Povlock, Clint Reach, Scott Boston, Samuel Charap, William Mackenzie, Katya Migacheva, Trevor Johnston, and Austin Long, *The Future of the Russian Military: Russia's Ground Combat Capabilities and Implications for U.S.-Russia Competition*, Santa Monica, Calif.: RAND Corporation, RR-3099-A, 2019. As of June 1, 2019:
https://www.rand.org/pubs/research_reports/RR3099.html

Raines, Thomas, Matthew Goodwin, and David Cutts, *The Future of Europe: Comparing Public and Elite Attitudes*, London: Chatham House, June 2017. As of July 18, 2018:
https://www.chathamhouse.org/publication/
future-europe-comparing-public-and-elite-attitudes

Ramirez, Carlos, "Abe's Trump Challenge and Japan's Foreign Policy Choices," *The Diplomat*, March 7, 2017. As of November 15, 2017:
https://thediplomat.com/2017/03/
abes-trump-challenge-and-japans-foreign-policy-choices

Rauhala, Emily, "Duterte Renounces U.S., Declares Philippines Will Embrace China," *Washington Post*, October 20, 2016. As of November 20, 2017: https://www.washingtonpost.com/world/philippines-duterte-saysgoodbye-washington-and-helloto-beijing/2016/10/20/865f3cd0-9571-11e6-9cae-2a3574e296a6_story.html?utm_term=.6d91b967c317

Renard, Thomas, and Rik Coolsaet, eds., *Returnees: Who Are They, Why Are They (Not) Coming Back and How Should We Deal with Them?* Brussels: Egmont Institute, February 2018. As of July 18, 2018: http://www.egmontinstitute.be/returnees-assessing-policies-on-returning-foreign-terrorist-fighters-in-belgium-germany-and-the-netherlands/

Rettman, Andrew, "Merkel: Nord Stream 2 Is 'Political,'" *EU Observer*, April 11, 2018a. As of July 18, 2018: https://euobserver.com/energy/141570

———, "Germany Starts to Build Nord Stream 2," *EU Observer*, May 4, 2018b. As of July 18, 2018: https://euobserver.com/foreign/141756

Reuters, "Which Countries Are Part of Saudi Arabia's Coalition Against Yemen's Houthis?" *Huffington Post*, March 26, 2015. As of September 5, 2018: https://www.huffingtonpost.com/2015/03/26/saudi-coalition-yemen_n_6946092.html

———, "China Deploys Cruise Missiles on South China Sea Outposts—Reports," *The Guardian*, May 3, 2018. As of May 14, 2018: https://www.theguardian.com/world/2018/may/03/china-deploys-cruise-missiles-on-south-china-sea-outposts-reports

"RF sdelaet vse, chtoby ne dopustit' prinjatija Ukrainy i Gruzii v NATO" ["Russian Federation Will Do Everything to Prevent Accession of Ukraine and Georgia to NATO"], *Ria Novosti*, April 8, 2008. As of February 2, 2018: https://ria.ru/politics/20080408/104075411.html

Rinehart, Ian E., and Bart Elias, *China's Air Defense Identification Zone (ADIZ),*" Washington, D.C.: Congressional Research Service, R43894, January 30, 2015.

Robinson, Linda, Todd C. Helmus, Raphael S. Cohen, Alireza Nader, Andrew Radin, Madeline Magnuson, and Katya Migacheva, *Modern Political Warfare: Current Practices and Possible Responses*, Santa Monica, Calif.: RAND Corporation, RR-1772-A, 2018. As of December 5, 2018: https://www.rand.org/pubs/research_reports/RR1772.html

Robinson, Thomas W., "The Sino-Soviet Border Dispute: Background, Development, and the March 1969 Clashes," *American Political Science Review*, Vol. 66, No. 4, 1972, pp. 1175–1202.

Rodkiewicz, Witold, "The Russian Attack on the United Kingdom: The Aims and Consequences," Warsaw: OSW Centre for Eastern Studies, March 14, 2018. As of July 18, 2018:
https://www.osw.waw.pl/en/publikacje/analyses/2018-03-14/russian-attack-united-kingdom-aims-and-consequences

Ross, Robert S., "The 1995–96 Taiwan Strait Confrontation: Coercion, Credibility, and the Use of Force," *International Security*, Vol. 25, No. 2, 2000, pp. 87–123.

Russell, John, *Chechnya-Russia's 'War on Terror,'* London: Routledge, 2007.

"Russian Spy: Highly Likely Moscow Behind Attack, Says Theresa May," BBC News, March 13, 2018. As of March 21, 2018:
http://www.bbc.com/news/uk-43377856

"S-400, Pantsir Air Defense Systems Protect Russian Air Group in Syria 24/7," *Sputnik*, April 7, 2017.

Saab, Bilal Y., "Don't Let the Saudis Destabilize Lebanon: Why Washington Should Restrain Riyadh," *Foreign Affairs*, November 20, 2017. As of December 6, 2017:
https://www.foreignaffairs.com/print/1121398

Sabochik, Katelyn, "President Obama on the Way Forward in Afghanistan," Obama White House Archives, June 22, 2011. As of November 9, 2017:
https://obamawhitehouse.archives.gov/blog/2011/06/22/president-obama-way-forward-afghanistan

Samaras, Antonis, "Syriza Is Undermining Democracy in Greece," *Financial Times*, March 8, 2018. As of July 18, 2018:
https://www.ft.com/content/950e7094-221e-11e8-8138-569c3d7ab0a7

Schanzer, Jonathan, "The Iran Deal's Bigger Loser: Hezbollah's Uncertain Future," *Foreign Affairs*, March 20, 2016. As of December 6, 2017:
https://www.foreignaffairs.com/print/1117027

Schwirtz, Michael, "Russia Ends Operations in Chechnya," *New York Times*, April 16, 2009.

Scobell, Andrew, *China's Use of Military Force: Beyond the Great Wall and the Long March*, New York: Cambridge University Press, 2003.

Sergeev, Dmitri, "Koshmarnyi son Tbilisi: kak otreagiruet Rossiya v sluchae agressii protiv Abkhazii" ["Tbilisi's Nightmare: How Russia Will React in Case of Aggression Against Abkhazia"], tvzvezda.ru, March 11, 2016. As of February 9, 2018:
https://tvzvezda.ru/news/vstrane_i_mire/content/201611030730-3uh5.htm

Serrano, Francisco, "Algeria on the Brink? Five Years After the Arab Spring," *Foreign Affairs*, May 27, 2017. As of December 11, 2017:
https://www.foreignaffairs.com/print/1117594

Shalal, Andrea, "Equipment Shortages Impair German Military Ahead of Key NATO Mission," Reuters, February 19, 2018. As of July 18, 2018: https://www.reuters.com/article/us-germany-military/equipment-shortages-impair-german-military-ahead-of-key-nato-mission-idUSKCN1G31PX

Shang-su, Wu, "Is Vietnam in Denial on Military Strategy?" *East Asia Forum*, October 30, 2014. As of November 15, 2017: http://www.eastasiaforum.org/2014/10/30/is-vietnam-in-denial-in-military-strategy/

Shatz, Howard J., and Nathan Chandler, *Global Economic Trends and the Future of Warfare: The Changing Global Environment and Its Implications for the U.S. Air Force*, Santa Monica, Calif.: RAND Corporation, RR-2849/4-AF, 2020. As of May 2020: https://www.rand.org/pubs/research_reports/RR2849z4.html

Shepard, Steven, "Poll: No Increase in Support for Military Action in North Korea," *Politico*, August 16, 2017. As of November 8, 2017: https://www.politico.com/story/2017/08/16/north-korea-trump-military-241671

"Shojgu: rasshirenie prisutstvija RF v Mirovom okeane trebuetsja iz-za nestabil'noj obstanovki" [Shoigu: Russia Should Expand Its Military Presence in the World Ocean Due to the Unstable (Security) Situation"], Tass.ru, October 27, 2017. As of March 20, 2018: http://tass.ru/armiya-i-opk/4682077

Simpson, Emile, "Theresa May Should Go After Putin's Debt," *Foreign Policy*, March 21, 2018. As of July 18, 2018: https://foreignpolicy.com/2018/03/21/theresa-may-should-go-after-putins-debt/

Sky, Emma, "Mission Still Not Accomplished in Iraq: Why the United States Should Not Leave," *Foreign Affairs*, October 16, 2017. As of December 11, 2017: https://www.foreignaffairs.com/print/1120968

Snyder, Jack, Robert Y. Shapiro, and Yaeli Bloch-Elkon, "Free Hand Abroad, Divide and Rule at Home," *World Politics*, Vol. 61, No. 1, January 2009, pp. 155–187.

Solov'ev, V., "Miroporyadok 2018" ["World Order 2018"], True TV, March 22, 2018. As of April 12, 2018: http://www.pravda-tv.ru/2018/03/19/348339/miroporyadok-2018-novyj-film-vladimira-soloveva-o-putine-smotret-video-onlajn

Spiegel, Peter, "Paris Attacks: Belgium Cries Foul over French Blame Game," *Financial Times*, November 18, 2015. As of July 18, 2018: https://www.ft.com/content/8bc3053e-8e57-11e5-a549-b89a1dfede9b

Srivastava, Mehul, and Erika Solomon, "Israel Launches Air Strikes Deep Within Syria," *Financial Times*, February 10, 2018. As of February 11, 2018: https://www.ft.com/content/7d79bbdc-0e41-11e8-8cb6-b9ccc4c4dbbb

State Council Information Office, "The One-China Principle and the Taiwan Issue," Beijing, government white paper, 2000. As of March 31, 2018: http://en.people.cn/features/taiwanpaper/taiwan.html

———, "China's Peaceful Development," Beijing, government white paper, 2011. As of March 31, 2018: http://www.scio.gov.cn/zfbps/ndhf/2011/Document/1000032/1000032_4.htm

———, *The Diversified Employment of China's Armed Forces*, Beijing, April 2013. As of April 10, 2018: http://eng.mod.gov.cn/Database/WhitePapers/2012.htm

———, *China's Military Strategy*, Beijing, May 2015. As of April 10, 2018: http://eng.mod.gov.cn/Database/WhitePapers/2014.htm

Strategiya natsional'noi bezopasnosti Rossiiskoi Federatsii [National Security Strategy of the Russian Federation], Decree of the President of the Russian Federation, No. 683, December 31, 2015. As of January 3, 2018: http://kremlin.ru/acts/bank/40391

Stueck, William, *The Korean War: An International History*, Princeton, N.J.: Princeton University Press, 1997.

Swaine, Michael D., Sara A. Daly, and Peter W. Greenwood, *Interpreting China's Grand Strategy: Past, Present, and Future*, Santa Monica, Calif.: RAND Corporation, MR-1121-AF, 2000. As of December 4, 2018: https://www.rand.org/pubs/monograph_reports/MR1121.html

Sweis, Rana F., "Jordan Struggles Under a Wave of Syrian Refugees," *New York Times*, February 13, 2016. As of December 14, 2017: https://www.nytimes.com/2016/02/14/world/middleeast/jordan-syria-refugees.html

Swift, Art, "1 in 3 Americans Say U.S. Spends Too Little on Defense," Gallup, March 2, 2017. As of November 7, 2017: http://news.gallup.com/poll/204782/americans-say-spends-little-defense.aspx

Szayna, Thomas S., Angela O'Mahony, Jennifer Kavanagh, Stephen Watts, Bryan Frederick, Tova C. Norlen, and Phoenix Voorhies, *Conflict Trends and Conflict Drivers: An Empirical Assessment of Historical Conflict Patterns and Future Conflict Projections*, Santa Monica, Calif.: RAND Corporation, RR-1063-A, 2017. As of October 24, 2018: https://www.rand.org/pubs/research_reports/RR1063.html

Takenaka, Kiyoshi, "Abe Hails 'Fresh Start' to Japan-China Ties After Xi Meeting," Reuters, November 11, 2017. As of November 15, 2017: https://www.reuters.com/article/us-apec-summit-japan-china/abe-hails-fresh-start-to-japan-china-ties-after-xi-meeting-idUSKBN1DB0HU

Techau, Jan, "Four Predictions on the Future of Europe," *Judy Dempsey's Strategic Europe*, Carnegie Europe blog, January 12, 2016. As of July 18, 2018: http://carnegieeurope.eu/strategiceurope/62445

Than, Krisztina, and Gabriela Baczynska, "Eastern EU States Tell Brussels to Back Off," Reuters, January 26, 2018. As of July 18, 2018:
https://www.reuters.com/article/us-europe-hungary-visegrad/eastern-eu-states-tell-brussels-to-back-off-idUSKBN1FF1U3

Thompson, Gavin, Oliver Hawkins, Aliyah Dar, Mark Taylor, Nick Battley, Adam Mellows-Facer, Chris Rhodes, Daniel Harari, Dominic Webb, Feargal McGuinness, Gavin Berman, Grahame Allen, Lorna Booth, Lucinda Maer, Matthew Keep, Nida Broughton, Paul Bolton, Rachael Harker, Richard Cracknell, Roderick McInnes, and Tom Rutherford, *Olympic Britain: Social and Economic Change Since the 1908 and 1948 London Games*, London: House of Commons Publications, 2012. As of July 18, 2018:
https://www.parliament.uk/documents/commons/lib/research/olympic-britain/olympicbritain.pdf

Thorne, Devin, and Ben Spevack, *Harbored Ambitions: How China's Port Investments Are Strategically Reshaping the Indo-Pacific*, Washington, D.C.: C4ADS, April 17, 2018. As of July 28, 2018:
https://static1.squarespace.com/static/566ef8b4d8af107232d5358a/t/5ad5e20ef950b777a94b55c3/1523966489456/Harbored+Ambitions.pdf

Thrall, A. Trevor, and Erik Goepner, *Millennials and U.S. Foreign Policy: The Next Generation's Attitudes Towards Foreign Policy and War (and Why They Matter)*, Washington, D.C.: Cato Institute, 2017. As of November 10, 2017:
https://object.cato.org/sites/cato.org/files/pubs/pdf/20150616_thrallgoepner_millennialswp.pdf

Torelli, Stefano M., "Ideology First: Italy's Troubled Approach to Migration," London, European Council on Foreign Relations, June 11, 2018. As of July 18, 2018:
https://www.ecfr.eu/article/commentary_ideology_first_italys_troubled_approach_to_migration

Tran, Pierre, and Andrew Chuter, "Domestic Response to Syria Strikes: Cheers in France, Lashing in UK," *Defense News*, April 16, 2018. As of July 18, 2018:
https://www.defensenews.com/global/europe/2018/04/17/domestic-response-to-syria-strikes-cheers-in-france-lashing-in-uk/

Trenin, Dmitrii, "Rossija na Blizhnem Vostoke: zadachi, prioritety, politicheskie stimuly" ["Russia in the Middle East: Tasks, Priorities, Political Incentives"], Moscow: Carnegie Moscow Center, April 21, 2016. As of February 3, 2018:
http://carnegie.ru/2016/04/21/ru-pub-63388

———, *Avoiding U.S.-Russia Military Escalation During the Hybrid War*, Moscow: Carnegie Endowment for International Peace, January 2018. As of March 3, 2018:
http://carnegieendowment.org/files/Trenin_Hybrid_War_web.pdf

Trump, Donald J., "Inaugural Address," White House website, January 2017a. As of November 9, 2017:
https://www.whitehouse.gov/inaugural-address

———, "Full Transcript: Trump Statement on Syria Strikes," via *Politico*, April 6, 2017b. As of November 9, 2017:
https://www.politico.com/story/2017/04/trump-syria-statement-transcript-236976

Tsygankov, Andrei P., *Russia's Foreign Policy: Change and Continuity in National Identity*, Lanham, Md.: Rowman & Littlefield, 2016.

Underwood, Alexia, "Sisi Won Egypt's Election. That Doesn't Mean He's Safe," Vox.com, April 3, 2018. As of September 4, 2018:
https://www.vox.com/2018/3/26/17033030/egypt-elections-results-sisi-president-trump

"Unraveling the Connections Among the Paris Attackers," *New York Times*, March 18, 2016. As of July 18, 2018:
https://www.nytimes.com/interactive/2015/11/15/world/europe/manhunt-for-paris-attackers.html

U.S.–China Economic and Security Review Commission, "Annual Reports," webpage, undated. As of April 20, 2018:
https://www.uscc.gov/Annual_Reports

U.S. Department of Defense, *Annual Report to Congress, Military and Security Developments Involving the People's Republic of China*, Washington, D.C., 2017.

———, *Summary of the 2018 National Defense Strategy of the United States: Sharpening American Military's Competitive Edge*, Washington, D.C., January 2018.

U.S. Department of State, Office of the Spokesperson, "Joint Statement on the Inaugural U.S.-India 2+2 Ministerial Dialogue," Washington, D.C., September 6, 2018. As of September 13, 2018:
https://www.state.gov/r/pa/prs/ps/2018/09/285729.htm

U.S. Energy Information Agency, "How Much Petroleum Does the United States Import and Export?" webpage, October 3, 2018. As of October 25, 2018:
https://www.eia.gov/tools/faqs/faq.php?id=727&t=6

U.S. Senate, Resolution 239, 90th Congress, 2nd session, June 11, 1948. As of November 6, 2017:
http://avalon.law.yale.edu/20th_century/decad040.asp

Vatanka, Alex, "Iran and Russia, Growing Apart: Rising Dissent over the IRGC's Militias," *Foreign Affairs*, November 29, 2017. As of December 6, 2017:
https://www.foreignaffairs.com/print/1121448

Vilmer, Jean-Baptiste Jeangene, and Olivier Schmitt, "Frogs of War: Explaining the New French Military Interventionism," *War on the Rocks*, October 4, 2015. As of July 18, 2018:
https://warontherocks.com/2015/10/frogs-of-war-explaining-the-new-french-military-interventionism/

von Clausewitz, Carl, *On War*, ed. and trans. Michael Howard and Peter Paret, Princeton, N.J.: Princeton University Press, 1984.

von Hammerstein, Konstantin, and Peter Muller, "U.S. Pressures Germany to Increase Defense Spending," *Spiegel Online*, February 17, 2017. As of July 18, 2018: http://www.spiegel.de/international/world/pressure-on-germany-to-increase-defense-spending-for-nato-a-1135192.html

Walsh, Alistair, "Chancellor Angela Merkel Rejects Refugee Limit for Germany in TV Interview," *Deutsche Welle*, July 16, 2017. As of July 18, 2018: https://www.dw.com/en/chancellor-angela-merkel-rejects-refugee-limit-for-germany-in-tv-interview/a-39714436

Wang, Yuan-Kang, *Harmony and War: Confucian Culture and Chinese Power Politics*, New York: Columbia University Press, 2010.

"Where Do EU Countries Stand on Migration?" *Deutsche Welle*, June 22, 2018. As of July 18, 2018: https://www.dw.com/en/where-do-eu-countries-stand-on-migration/a-44356857

White House, Office of the Press Secretary, "U.S.-India Joint Strategic Vision for the Asia-Pacific and Indian Ocean Region," Washington, D.C., January 25, 2015. As of November 28, 2017: https://obamawhitehouse.archives.gov/the-press-office/2015/01/25/us-india-joint-strategic-vision-asia-pacific-and-indian-ocean-region

Whiting, Allen Suess, *China Crosses the Yalu: The Decision to Enter the Korean War*, Palo Alto, Calif.: Stanford University Press, 1968.

Wike, Richard, Bruce Stokes, and Katie Simmons, "Europeans Fear Wave of Refugees Will Mean More Terrorism, Fewer Jobs," Pew Research Center, July 11, 2016. As of July 18, 2018: http://www.pewglobal.org/2016/07/11/europeans-fear-wave-of-refugees-will-mean-more-terrorism-fewer-jobs/

Williams, Aaron, "How Two Brussels Neighborhoods Became 'a Breeding Ground' for Terror," *Washington Post*, April 1, 2016. As of July 18, 2018: https://www.washingtonpost.com/graphics/world/brussels-molenbeek-demographics/

Windsor, Jennifer L., "Promoting Democratization Can Combat Terrorism," *Washington Quarterly*, Vol. 26, No. 3, 2003, pp. 43–58.

Worldwide Independent Network/Gallup International, "WIN/Gallup International's Global Survey Shows Three in Five Willing to Fight for Their Country," webpage, 2015. As of July 18, 2018: http://gallup-international.bg/en/Publications/2015/220-WIN-Gallup-International%E2%80%99s-global-survey-shows-three-in-five-willing-to-fight-for-their-country

Wuthnow, Joel, and Phillip Charles Saunders, *Chinese Military Reform in the Age of Xi Jinping: Drivers, Challenges, and Implications*, Washington, D.C.: National Defense University Press, 2017.

"Xi Jinping Attends PLA Delegation Plenary Meeting" ["习近平出席解放军代表团全体会议"], *People's Daily* [人民日报], March 11, 2014. As of March 27, 2018: http://lianghui.people.com.cn/2014npc/n/2014/0312/c376707-24609511.html

Yerkes, Sarah E., "Democracy Derailed? Tunisia's Transition Veers Off Course," *Foreign Affairs*, October 2, 2017. As of December 8, 2017: https://www.foreignaffairs.com/print/1121008

YouGov, "61% Oppose Sending U.S. Ground Troops to Libya," Economist/YouGov Poll, June 10, 2011. As of November 8, 2017: https://today.yougov.com/news/2011/06/10/61-oppose-sending-us-ground-troops-libya/

Yufan, Hao, and Zhai Zhihai, "China's Decision to Enter the Korean War: History Revisited," *China Quarterly*, Vol. 121, 1990, pp. 94–115.

Zakharov, Vladimir, "Sostoyanie i perspektivy razvitiya Organizatsii Dogovora o kollektivnoi bezopasnosti" ["The State and Development Prospects of the Collective Security Treaty Organization"], *PROBLEMY NATSIONAL'OI STRATEGII [Problems and National Strategies]*, Vol. 3, No. 12, 2012, pp. 84–97.

Zanotti, Jim, and Clayton Thomas, *Turkey: Background and U.S. Relations in Brief*, Washington, D.C.: Congressional Research Service, R44000, November 9, 2017. As of December 11, 2017: https://www.hsdl.org/?view&did=805908